Withdrawn

Illinois Central College
Learning Resource Center

GRANGERS

Our Holidays in Poetry

FRONTISPIECE *by Jeannette C. Shirk*

Our Holidays in Poetry

COMPILED BY

MILDRED P. HARRINGTON, *1886 -*

JOSEPHINE H. THOMAS

and

A COMMITTEE OF THE CARNEGIE
LIBRARY SCHOOL ASSOCIATION

NEW YORK
THE H. W. WILSON COMPANY
1929

Published 1929

Second Printing 1935

Third Printing 1938

Fourth Printing 1945

Fifth Printing 1950

Sixth Printing 1956

Seventh Printing 1961

Eighth Printing 1965

Ninth Printing 1968

Printed in the United States of America

Library of Congress Catalog Card No. 29-26163

PREFACE

In our library work with children it has been difficult to find holiday poems, including the more modern poems, which both have literary merit and are easily comprehensible to children.

The present volume, compiled from the series of holiday poetry booklets, is an attempt to meet this need.

The proceeds derived from the publication of both book and booklets are used to increase the Student Loan Fund of the Carnegie Library School Association.

We are most grateful to the authors and publishers who have so generously permitted copyright material to be used, to Miss Dorothy Grout, who has given so freely of her time and effort and to Miss Elva S. Smith, former president of the Association for her valued advice and help.

The members of the poetry committee, whose careful work and interest in this undertaking have made the compilation possible, are as follows: Mary Wilkinson, Jasmine Britton, Dorothy Grout, Grace Darling, Alice Stoeltzing and Dorothy Hayes.

MILDRED P. HARRINGTON
Chairman of the Poetry Committee
Carnegie Library School Association

CONTENTS

CONTENTS

EASTER IN POETRY

CONTENTS

ARBOR DAY IN POETRY

CONTENTS

MOTHER'S DAY IN POETRY

x

CONTENTS

MEMORIAL DAY IN POETRY

CONTENTS

THANKSGIVING IN POETRY

CONTENTS

CHRISTMAS IN POETRY

CONTENTS

LINCOLN IN POETRY

This man whose homely face you look upon,
    Was one of nature's masterful, great men;
Born with strong arms, that unfought battles won;
    Direct of speech, and cunning with the pen.
Chosen for large designs, he had the art
    Of winning with his humor, and he went
Straight to his mark, which was the human heart;
    Wise, too, for what he could not break, he bent!

Richard Henry Stoddard

ABRAHAM LINCOLN

Born in a hovel, trained in Hardship's school,
He rose sublime, a conqueror over all.
His life of labor, thought and burden-bearing
Brought forth his kingly qualities of soul.
Upon his lofty brow he wore those crowns
Which only come with suffering and toil,
The crowns of wisdom, strength and God-like love
For all mankind, both enemies and friends.
His spirit still is with us in our need;
His work goes on increasing through all time.

A. S. Ames

Included by permission of the Palmer Company, Publishers.

ABRAHAM LINCOLN

Whence came this man? As if on the wings
    Of the winds of God that blew!
He moved, undaunted, mid captains and kings,
    And, not having learned, he knew!
Was he son of the soil, or child of the sky?
    Or, pray, was he both? Ah me!
How little they dreamed, as the storm rolled nigh,
    What he was, and was to be!

When trembled the lamps of hope, or quite
    Blew out in that furious gale,
He drew his light from the Larger Light
    Above him that did not fail:
Heaven-led, all trials and perils among,
    As unto some splendid goal
He fared right onward, unflinching—this strong,
    God-gifted, heroic soul!

We know him now—how noble his part,
    And how clear was his vision then!
With the firmest hand and the kindliest heart
    Of them all—this master of men!
Of the pride of power or the lust of pelf,
    Oh, never a taint we find:
He lost himself in the larger self
    Of his country and all mankind.

There are those called great, or good, by right,
    But as long as the long roll is,
Not many the names, with the double light
    Of greatness and goodness, like his.
Thrice happy the nation that holds him dear
    Who never can wholly die,
Never cease to bestow of his counsel and cheer,
    As the perilous years go by!

ABRAHAM LINCOLN

For after the trumpets have ceased to blow,
    And the banners are folded away,
And the stress and the splendor forgotten, we know,
    Of a truth, in that judgment day,
That whatso'er else, in the Stream that rolls,
    May sink and be utterly gone,
The souls of the men who were true to their souls
      Forever go marching on!

There are those whose like, it was somehow planned,
    We never again shall see;
But I would to God there were more in the land
    As true and as simple as he,—
As he who walked in our common ways,
    With the seal of a king on his brow;
Who lived as a man among men his days,
    And belongs to the ages now!

Samuel Valentine Cole

Included by permission of William I. Cole.

ABRAHAM LINCOLN

This man whose homely face you look upon,
    Was one of nature's masterful, great men;
Born with strong arms, that unfought battles won;
    Direct of speech, and cunning with the pen.

Chosen for large designs, he had the art
    Of winning with his humor, and he went
Straight to his mark, which was the human heart;
    Wise, too, for what he could not break, he bent.

Upon his back a more than Atlas-load,
    The burden of the Commonwealth, was laid;
He stooped, and rose up to it, though the road
    Shot suddenly downwards, not a whit dismayed.
Hold, warriors, councillors, kings! All now give
      place
To this dear Benefactor of the race.

Richard Henry Stoddard

Included by permission of Charles Scribner's Sons.

ABRAHAM LINCOLN, THE MASTER

We need him now—his rugged faith that held
Fast to the rock of Truth through all the days
Of moil and strife, the sleepless nights; upheld
By very God was he—that God who stays
All hero-souls who will but trust in Him,
And trusting, labor as if God were not.
His eyes beheld the stars, clouds could not dim
Their glory; but his task was not forgot—
To keep his people one; to hold them true
To that fair dream their fathers willed to them—

6

ABRAHAM LINCOLN

Freedom for all; to spur them; to renew
Their hopes in bitter days; strife to condemn.
Such was his task, and well his work was done—
Who willed us greater tasks, when set his sun.

Thomas Curtis Clark

Included by permission of the author.

ABRAHAM LINCOLN WALKS AT MIDNIGHT

It is portentous, and a thing of state
　　That here at midnight, in our little town
A mourning figure walks, and will not rest,
　　Near the old courthouse pacing up and down.

Or by his homestead, or in shadowed yards.
　　He lingers where his children used to play,
Or through the market, on the well-worn stones
　　He stalks until the dawn-stars burn away.

A bronzed, lank man! His suit of ancient black,
　　A famous high-top hat and plain worn shawl
Make him the quaint great figure that men love,
　　The prairie lawyer, master of us all.

He cannot sleep upon his hillside now.
　　He is among us;—as in times before!
And we who toss and lie awake for long
　　Breathe deep, and start, to see him pass the door.

His head is bowed. He thinks on men and kings.
    Yea, when the sick world cries, how can he sleep?
Too many peasants fight, they know not why,
    Too many homesteads in black terror weep.

The sins of all the war-lords burn his heart.
    He sees the dreadnoughts scouring every main.
He carries on his shawl-wrapped shoulders now
    The bitterness, the folly and the pain.

                              Vachel Lindsay

From "Collected Poems" by Vachel Lindsay.
Included by permission of The Macmillan Company.

CENOTAPH OF LINCOLN

And so they buried Lincoln? Strange and vain,
    Has any creature thought of Lincoln hid
    In any vault 'neath any coffin lid,
In all the years since that wild spring of pain?
'Tis false—he never in the grave hath lain.
    You could not bury him although you slid
    Upon his clay the Cheops Pyramid,
Or heaped it with the Rocky Mountain chain,
They slew themselves;—they but set Lincoln free,
    In all the earth his great heart beats as strong,

Shall beat while pulses throb to chivalry,
    And burn with hate of tyranny and wrong,
Whoever will may find him, anywhere
Save in the tomb. Not there—he is not there.

James T. McKay

Included by permission of Century Company.

FROM "THE GETTYSBURG ODE"

After the eyes that looked, the lips that spake
Here, from the shadows of impending death,
    Those words of solemn breath,
    What voice may fitly break
The silence doubly hallowed, left by him?
We can but bow the head, with eyes grown dim,
    And as a Nation's litany, repeat
The phrase his martyrdom hath made complete,
Noble as then, but now more sadly sweet:
"Let us, the Living, rather dedicate
Ourselves to the unfinished work, which they
Thus far advanced so nobly on its way,
    And saved the perilled State!
Let us, upon this field where they, the brave,
Their last full measure of devotion gave,
Highly resolve they have not died in vain!—

9

That, under God, the Nation's later birth
    Of Freedom, and the people's gain
Of their own Sovereignty, shall never wane
And perish from the circle of the earth!"
From such a perfect text, shall Song aspire
       To light her faded fire,
    And in wandering music turn
Its virtue, simple, sorrowful and stern!
His voice all elegies anticipated;
      For, whatsoe'er the strain,
      We hear that one refrain:
"We consecrate ourselves to them, the Consecrated!"

Bayard Taylor

Included by permission of Houghton Mifflin Company.

THE HAND OF LINCOLN

Look on this cast, and know the hand
    That bore a nation in its hold;
From this mute witness understand
    What Lincoln was—how large of mold.

The man who sped the woodman's team,
    And deepest sunk the plowman's share,
And pushed the laden raft astream,
    Of fate before him unaware.

10

ABRAHAM LINCOLN

This was the hand that knew to swing
    The axe—since thus would Freedom train
Her son—and made the forest ring,
    And drove the wedge, and toiled amain.

Firm hand, that loftier office took,
    A conscious leader's will obeyed,
And, when men sought his word and look,
    With steadfast might the gathering swayed

No courtier's, toying with a sword,
    Nor minstrel's, laid across a lute;
A chief's, uplifted to the Lord
    When all the kings of earth were mute!

The hand of Anak, sinewed strong,
    The fingers that on greatness clutch;
Yet, lo! the marks their lines along
    Of one who strove and suffered much.

For here in knotted cord and vein,
    I trace the varying chart of years;
I know the troubled heart, the strain,
    The weight of Atlas—and the tears.

Again I see the patient brow
    That palm erewhile was wont to press;
And now 'tis furrowed deep, and now
    Made smooth with hope and tenderness.

For something of a formless grace
   This molded outline plays about;
A pitying flame, beyond our trace,
   Breathes like a spirit, in and out.

The love that casts an aureole
   Round one who, longer to endure,
Called mirth to ease his ceaseless dole,
   Yet kept his nobler purpose sure.

Lo, as I gaze, the statured man,
   Built up from yon large hand, appears;
A type that nature wills to plan
   But once in all a people's years.

What better than this voiceless cast
   To tell of such a one as he,
Since through its living semblance passed
   The thought that bade a race be free.

Edmund Clarence Stedman

Included by permission of Houghton Mifflin Company.

HE LEADS US STILL

Dare we despair? Through all the nights and days
   Of lagging war he kept his courage true
Shall Doubt befog our eyes? A darker haze
   But proved the faith of him who ever knew

ABRAHAM LINCOLN

That Right must conquer.   May we cherish hate
    For our poor griefs, when never word nor deed
Of rancor, malice, spite, of low or great,
    In his large soul one poison drop could breed?

He leads us still.   O'er chasms yet unspanned
    Our pathway lies; the work is but begun;
But we shall do our part and leave our land
    The mightier for noble battles won.
Here Truth must triumph, Honor must prevail;
    The Nation Lincoln died for cannot fail!

Arthur Guiterman

Revised by the author.
From "A Ballad-Maker's Pack" by Arthur Guiterman, published by
   Harper Brothers. Included by permission of the author.

A HERO

He sang of joy; whate'er he knew of sadness
    He kept for his own heart's peculiar share:
So well he sang, the world imagined gladness
    To be sole tenant there.

For dreams were his, and in the dawn's fair shining,
    His spirit soared beyond the mounting lark;
But from his lips no accent of repining
    Fell when the days grew dark;

13

And though contending long dread Fate to master,
 He failed at last her enmity to cheat,
He turned with such a smile to face disaster
 That he sublimed defeat.

Florence Earle Coates

Included by permission of the author and Harper Brothers.

HIS FACE

They tell you Lincoln was ungainly, plain?
 To some he seemed so; true.
Yet in his look was charm to gain
 E'en such as I, who knew
With how confirmed a will he tried
To overthrow a cause for which I would have died.

The sun may shine with naught to shroud
 Its beam, yet show less bright
Than when from out eclipsing cloud
 It pours its radiant light;
And Lincoln, seen amid the shows of war
Clothed in his sober black, was somehow felt the more

To be a centre and a soul of power—
 An influence benign
To kindle in a faithless hour
 New trust in the divine.

14

ABRAHAM LINCOLN

Grave was his visage, but no cloud could dull
The radiance from within that made it beautiful.

A prisoner, when I saw him first—
    Wounded and sick for home—
His presence soothed my yearning's thirst
    While yet his lips were dumb;
For such compassion as his countenance wore
I had not seen nor felt in human face before.

And when, low-bending o'er his foe,
    He took in his firm hand
My wasted one, I seemed to know
    We two were of one Land;
And as my cheek flushed warm with young surprise,
God's pity looked on me from Lincoln's sorrowing eyes.

His prisoner I was from then—
    Love makes surrender sure—
And though I saw him not again,
    Some memories endure,
And I am glad my untaught worship knew
His the divinest face I ever looked into!

Florence Earle Coates

Included by permission of the author and Harper Brothers.

HUSH'D BE THE CAMPS TO-DAY
(May 4, 1865)

Hush'd be the camps to-day,
And soldiers, let us drape our war-worn weapons,
And each with musing soul retire to celebrate
Our dear commander's death.

No more for him life's stormy conflicts,
Nor victory, nor defeat—no more time's dark events,
Charging like ceaseless clouds across the sky.

But sing, poet, in our name,
Sing of the love we bore him—because you, dweller in
    camps, know it truly.

As they invault the coffin there,
Sing—as they close the doors of earth upon him—one
    verse,
For the heavy hearts of soldiers.

Walt Whitman

Included by permission of David McKay Company.

LINCOLN

Lincoln! When men would name a man,
    Just, unperturbed, magnanimous,
Tried in the lowest seat of all,
    Tried in the chief seat of the house—

Lincoln! When men would name a man
    Who wrought the great work of his age,
Who fought and fought the noblest fight,
    And marshaled it from stage to stage.

Victorious, out of dusk and dark,
    And into dawn and on till day,
Most humble when the paeans rang,
    Least rigid when the enemy lay

Prostated for his feet to tread—
    This name of Lincoln will they name,
A name revered, a name of scorn,
    Of scorn to sundry, not to fame.

Lincoln, the man who freed the slave;
    Lincoln whom never self enticed;
Slain Lincoln, worthy found to die
    A soldier of his Captain Christ.

                                        Anonymous

17

LINCOLN

I knew the man.   I see him, as he stands
With gifts of mercy in his outstretched hands;
A kindly light within his gentle eyes,
Sad as the toil in which his heart grew wise;
His lips half-parted with the constant smile
That kindled truth, but foiled the deepest guile;
His head bent forward, and his willing ear
Divinely patient right and wrong to hear:
Great in his goodness, humble in his state,
Firm in his purpose, yet not passionate,
He led his people with a tender hand,
And won by love a sway beyond command,
Summoned by lot to mitigate a time
Frenzied by rage, unscrupulous with crime,
He bore his mission with so meek a heart
That Heaven itself took up his people's part,
And when he faltered, helped him ere he fell,
Eking his efforts out by miracle.
No King this man, by grace of God's intent;
No, something better, freeman,—President!
A nature, modeled on a higher plan,
Lord of himself, an inborn gentleman!

George Henry Boker

LINCOLN

The hour was on us; where the man?
The fateful sands unfaltering ran,
　　And up the way of tears
　　He came into the years.

Our pastoral captain.   Forth he came,
As one that answers to his name;
　　Nor dreamed how high his charge,
　　His work how fair and large,—

To set the stones back in the wall
Lest the divided house should fall,
　　And peace from men depart,
　　Hope and the childlike heart.

We looked on him; " 'Tis he," we said,
"Come crownless and unheralded,
　　The shepherd who will keep
　　The flocks, will fold the sheep."

Unknightly, yes; yet 'twas the mien
Presaging the immortal scene,
　　Some battle of His wars
　　Who sealeth up the stars.

Not he would take the past between
His hands, wipe valor's tablets clean.
　　Commanding greatness wait
　　Till he stand at the gate;

Not he would cramp to one small head
The awful laurels of the dead,
    Time's mighty vintage cup,
    And drink all honor up.

No flutter of the banners bold
Borne by the lusty sons of old,
    The haughty conquerors
    Set forward to their wars;
Not his their blare, their pageantries,
Their goal, their glory, was not his;
    Humbly he came to keep
    The flocks, to fold the sheep.

The need comes not without the man;
The prescient hours unceasing ran,
    And up the way of tears
    He came into the years.

Our pastoral captain, skilled to crook
The spear into the pruning hook,
    The simple, kindly man,
    Lincoln, American.

John Vance Cheney

Included by permission of The Independent.

ABRAHAM LINCOLN

LINCOLN

FATE struck the hour!
—A crisis hour of Time.
The tocsin of a people clanging forth
Thro' the wild South and thro' the startled North
Called for a leader, master of his kind,
Fearless and firm, with clear foreseeing mind;
Who should not flinch from calumny or scorn,
Who in the depth of night could ken the morn;
      Wielding a giant power
      Humbly, with faith sublime.
God knew the man His sovereign grace had sealed;
God touched the man, and Lincoln stood revealed!

Jane L. Hardy

Included by permission of The Outlook.

LINCOLN

Would I might rouse the Lincoln in you all,
That which is gendered in the wilderness
From lonely prairies and God's tenderness.
Imperial soul, star of a weedy stream,
Born where the ghosts of buffaloes still dream,
Whose spirit hoof-beats storm above his grave,
Above that breast of earth and prairie-fire—
Fire that freed the slave.

Vachel Lindsay

From "The Litany of the Heroes" in "Collected Poems" by Vachel Lindsay.
Included by permission of the author and The Macmillan Company.

21

LINCOLN

A peaceful life,—just toil and rest—
    All his desire;—
To read the books he liked the best
    Beside the cabin fire—
God's word and man's;—to peer sometimes
    Above the page, in smouldering gleams,
And catch, like far heroic rhymes,
    The monarch of his dreams.

A peaceful life;—to hear the low
    Of pastured herds,
Or woodman's axe that, blow on blow,
    Fell sweet as rhythmic words.
And yet there stirred within his breast
    A fateful pulse that, like a roll
Of drums, made high above his rest
    A tumult in his soul.

A peaceful life! . . . They hailed him even
    As one was hailed
Whose open palms were nailed toward Heaven
    When prayers nor aught availed.
And, lo, he paid the selfsame price
    To lull a nation's awful strife

ABRAHAM   LINCOLN

And will us, through the sacrifice
   Of self, his peaceful life.

James Whitcomb Riley

From "Home Folks." Copyright 1900.
Used by special permission of the publishers, The Bobbs-Merrill Co.

LINCOLN

A martyred Saint, he lies upon his bier,
While, with one heart, the kneeling nation weeps,
Until across the world the knowledge sweeps
That every sad and sacrificial tear
Waters the seed to patriot mourners dear,
That flowers in love of Country.   He who reaps
The gift of martyrdom, forever keeps
His soul in love of man, and God's own fear.
Great Prototype benign of Brotherhood—
Incarnate of the One who walked the shore
Of lonely lakes in distant Galilee;
With patient purpose undismayed he stood,
Steadfast and unafraid, and calmly bore
A Nation's Cross to a new Calvary!

Corinne Roosevelt Robinson

Included by permission of the author and Charles Scribner's Sons.

LINCOLN LEADS

Across the page of history,
    As in a looking-glass,
Or on a moving-picture screen,
    The nation's heroes pass;
With sword and mace and pen they pace
    In epaulets and braid,
And some, with ruffles at their wrists,
    In linen fine arrayed.

But at the long procession's head,
    In loose, ill-fitting clothes,
A lanky woodsman with an axe
    Upon his shoulder goes;
In every patriotic heart
    The figure lean and tall
Is shrined beside the starry flag,
    For Lincoln leads them all.

Minna Irving

Included by permission of the author.

THE LINCOLN STATUE
(*Gutzon Borglum, Sculptor*)

A man who drew his strength from all
    Because of all a part;
He led with wisdom, for he knew
    The common heart.

Its hopes, its fears his eye discerned,
    And, reading, he could share.
Its griefs were his, its burdens were
    For him to bear.
Its faith that wrong must sometime yield,
    That right is ever right,
Sustained him in the saddest hour,
    The darkest night.

In patient confidence he wrought,
    The people's will his guide,
Nor brought to his appointed task
    The touch of pride.

The people's man, familiar friend,
    Shown by the sculptor's art
As one who trusted, one who knew
    The common heart.

W. F. Collins

Included by permission of the author.

25

LINCOLN, THE MAN OF THE PEOPLE

When the Norn Mother saw the Whirlwind Hour
Greatening and darkening as it hurried on,
She left the Heaven of Heroes and came down
To make a man to meet the mortal need.
She took the tried clay of the common road—
Clay warm yet with the genial heat of Earth,
Dasht through it all a strain of prophecy;
Tempered the heap with thrill of human tears;
Then mixt a laughter with the serious stuff.
Into the shape she breathed a flame to light
That tender, tragic, ever-changing face;
And laid on him a sense of the Mystic Powers,
Moving—all husht—behind the mortal vail.
Here was a man to hold against the world,
A man to match the mountains and the sea.

The color of the ground was in him, the red earth;
The smack and tang of elemental things;
The rectitude and patience of the cliff;
The good-will of the rain that loves all leaves;
The friendly welcome of the wayside well;
The courage of the bird that dares the sea;
The gladness of the wind that shakes the corn:
The pity of the snow that hides all scars;

ABRAHAM LINCOLN

The secrecy of streams that make their way
Under the mountain to the rifted rock;
The tolerance and equity of light
That gives as freely to the shrinking flower
As to the great oak flaring to the wind—
To the grave's low hill as to the Matterhorn
That shoulders out the sky. Sprung from the West,
He drank the valorous youth of a new world.
The strength of virgin forests braced his mind,
The hush of spacious prairies stilled his soul,
His words were oaks in acorns; and his thoughts
Were roots that firmly gript the granite truth.

Up from log cabin to the Capitol,
One fire was on his spirit, one resolve—
To send the keen ax to the root of wrong,
Clearing a free way for the feet of God,
The eyes of conscience testing every stroke,
To make his deed the measure of a man,
He built the rail-pile as he built the State,
Pouring his splendid strength through every blow;
The grip that swung the ax in Illinois
Was on the pen that set a people free.

So came the Captain with the mighty heart;
And when the judgment thunders split the house,
Wrenching the rafters from their ancient rest,
He held the ridgepole up, and spikt again

The rafters of the Home. He held his place—
Held the long purpose like a growing tree—
Held on through blame and faltered not at praise—
Held on in calm rough-hewn sublimity,
And when he fell in whirlwind, he went down
As when a lordly cedar, green with boughs,
Goes down with a great shout upon the hills,
And leaves a lonesome place against the sky.

Edwin Markham

THE MAN OF PEACE

What winter holiday is this?
 In Time's great calendar,
Marked with the rubric of the saints,
 And with a soldier's star,
Here stands the name of one who lived
 To serve the common weal,
With humour, tender as a prayer
 And honour firm as steel.

No hundred hundred years can dim
 The radiance of his birth,
That set unselfish laughter free
 From all the sons of earth.

28

ABRAHAM   LINCOLN

Unswerved through stress and scant success,
    Out of his dreamful youth
He kept an unperverted faith
    In the almighty truth.

Born in the fulness of the days,
    Up from the teeming soil,
By the world-mother reared and schooled
    In reverence and toil,
He stands the test of all life's best
    Through play, defeat, or strain;
Never a moment was he found
    Unlovable nor vain.

Fondly we set apart this day,
    And mark this plot of earth
To be forever hallowed ground
    In honour of his birth,
Where men may come as to a shrine
    And temple of the good,
To be made sweet and strong of heart
    In Lincoln's brotherhood.

.   .   .   .   .   *Bliss Carman*
                              (Selected)

Included by permission of the author.

THE MASTER

A flying word from here and there
Had sown the name at which we sneered,
But soon the name was everywhere,
To be reviled and then revered:
A presence to be loved and feared,
We cannot hide it, or deny
That we, the gentlemen who jeered,
May be forgotten by and by.

He came when days were perilous
And hearts of men were sore beguiled;
And having made his note of us,
He pondered and was reconciled.
Was ever master yet so mild
As he, and so untamable?
We doubted, even when he smiled,
Not knowing what he did so well.

He knew that undeceiving fate
Would shame us whom he served unsought,
He knew that he must wince and wait—
The jest of those for whom he fought;
He knew devoutly what he thought
Of us and of our ridicule;
He knew that we must all be taught
Like little children in a school.

30

ABRAHAM LINCOLN

We have a glamour to the task
That he encountered and saw through,
But little of us did he ask,
And little did we ever do.
And what appears if we review
The season when we railed and chaffed?
It is the face of one who knew
That we were learning while we laughed.

The face that in our vision feels
Again the venom that we flung,
Transfigured to the world reveals
The vigilance to which we clung.
Shrewd, hallowed, harassed, and among
The mysteries that are retold,
The face we see was ever young,
Nor could it ever have been old.

For he, to whom we have applied
Our shopman's test of age and worth,
Was elemental when he died,
As he was ancient at his birth:
The saddest among kings of earth,
Bowed with a galling crown, this man
Met rancor with a cryptic mirth,
Laconic—and Olympian.

The love, the grandeur, and the fame
Are bounded by the world alone;
The calm, the smouldering, and the flame
Of awful patience were his own:
With him they are forever flown
Past all our fond self-shadowings,
Wherewith we cumber the Unknown
As with inept Icarian wings.

For we were not as other men:
'Twas ours to soar and his to see.
But we are coming down again,
And we shall come down pleasantly;
Nor shall we longer disagree
On what it is to be sublime,
But flourish in our perigee
And have one Titan at a time.

Edwin Arlington Robinson.

Included by permission of the author and Charles Scribner's Sons.

NANCY HANKS

Prairie child,
    Brief as dew,
What winds of wonder
    Nourished you?

ABRAHAM LINCOLN

Rolling plains
    Of billowy green;
Far horizons,
    Blue, serene;

Lofty skies
    The slow clouds climb,
Where burning stars
    Beat out the time:

These, and the dreams
    Of fathers bold—
Baffled longings,
    Hopes untold—

Gave to you
    A heart of fire,
Love like deep waters,
    Brave desire.

Ah, when youth's rapture
    Went out in pain,
And all seemed over,
    Was all in vain?

O soul obscure,
    Whose wings life bound,
And soft death folded
    Under the ground.

Wilding lady,
    Still and true,
Who gave us Lincoln
    And never knew:

To you at last
    Our praise, our tears.
Love and a song
    Through the nation's years.

Mother of Lincoln,
    Our tears, our praise;
A battle-flag
    And the victor's bays!

Harriet Monroe

Revised by the author.
Included by permission of the author and The Macmillan Company.

O CAPTAIN! MY CAPTAIN

O Captain! my Captain! our fearful trip is done,
The ship has weather'd every rock, the prize we sought
                is won,
The port is near, the bells I hear, the people all
                exulting,
While follow eyes the steady keel, the vessel grim and
                daring;

34

ABRAHAM   LINCOLN

But O heart! heart! heart!
O the bleeding drops of blood,
Where on the deck my Captain lies,
Fallen cold and dead.

O Captain! my Captain! rise up and hear the bells;
Rise up—for you the flag is flung—for you the bugle
trills.
For you bouquets and ribbon'd wreaths—for you the
shores a-crowding,
For you they call, the swaying mass, their eager faces
turning;
Here, Captain! dear father!
This arm beneath your head!
It is some dream that on the deck,
You've fallen cold and dead.

My Captain does not answer, his lips are pale and still,
My father does not feel my arm, he has no pulse nor
will,
The ship is anchor'd safe and sound, its voyage closed
and done,
From fearful trip the victor comes in with object won;
Exult, O shores, and ring, O bells!
But I with mournful tread,
Walk the deck my Captain lies,
Fallen cold and dead.

Walt Whitman

Included by permission of David McKay Company.

ON A BUST OF LINCOLN

This was a man of mighty mould
    Who walked erewhile our earthly ways,
Fashioned as leaders were of old
    In the heroic days!

Mark how austere the rugged height
    Of brow—a will not wrought to bend
Yet in the eyes behold the light
    That made the foe a friend!

Sagacious he beyond the test
    Of quibbling schools that praise or ban;
Supreme in all the broadest, best,
    We hail American.

When bronze is but as ash to flame,
    And marble but as wind-blown chaff,
Still shall the lustre of his name
    Stand as his cenotaph!

Clinton Scollard

Included by permission of the author.

OUR MARTYR-CHIEF

Such was he, our Martyr-Chief,
    Whom late the Nation he had led,
    With ashes on her head,
Wept with the passion of an angry grief:
Forgive me, if from present things I turn
To speak what in my heart will beat and burn,
And hang my wreath on his world-honored urn.
    Nature, they say, doth dote,
    And cannot make a man
    Save on some worn-out plan,
    Repeating up by rote;
For him her Old World moulds aside she threw,
    And, choosing sweet clay from the breast
    Of the unexhausted West,
With stuff untainted shaped a hero new,
Wise, steadfast in the strength of God, and true.
    How beautiful to see,
Once more a shepherd of mankind indeed,
Who loved his charge, but never loved to lead;
One whose meek flock the people joyed to be,
    Not lured by any cheat of birth,
    But by his clear-grained human worth,
And brave old wisdom of sincerity!
    They knew that outward grace is dust;
    They could not choose but trust

In the sure-footed mind's unfaltering skill,
    And supple-tempered will
That bent like perfect steel to spring again and thrust
    His was no lonely mountain-peak of mind,
Thrusting to thin air o'er our cloudy bars,
    A sea-mark now, now lost in vapors blind;
    Broad prairie rather, genial, level-lined,
    Fruitful and friendly for all human kind,
Yet also nigh to heaven and loved of loftiest stars.
Great captains, with their guns and drums,
Disturb our judgment for the hour,
    But at last silence comes;
These all are gone, and standing like a tower,
    Our children shall behold his fame,
    The kindly-earnest, brave, foreseeing man,
Sagacious, patient, dreading praise, not blame,
New birth of our new soil, the first American.

James Russell Lowell

Included by permission of Houghton Mifflin Company.

PRESIDENT LINCOLN'S GRAVE

    Lay his dear ashes where ye will,—
    On southern slope or western hill;
    And build above his sacred name
    Your proudest monument of fame;
    Yet still his grave our hearts shall be;

ABRAHAM LINCOLN

His monument a people free!
   Sing sweet, sing low!
   We loved him so!
His grave a nation's heart shall be,
His monument a people free!

Wave, prairie winds! above his sleep
Your mournful dirges, long and deep;
Proud marble! o'er his virtues raise
The tribute of your glittering praise;
Yet still his grave our hearts shall be;
His monument a people free!
   Sing sweet, sing low;
   We loved him so!
His grave a nation's heart shall be;
His monument a people free!

So just, so merciful, so wise,
Ye well may shrine him where he lies;
So simply good, so great the while
Ye well may praise the marble pile;
Yet still his grave our hearts shall be;
His monument a people free!
   Sing sweet, sing low;
   We loved him so!
His grave a nation's heart shall be;
His monument a people free!

Caroline A. Mason

TO BORGLUM'S SEATED STATUE
OF ABRAHAM LINCOLN

Alone, upon the broad low bench, he sits,
From carping foes and friends alike withdrawn;
With tragic patience for the spirit dawn
He waits, yet through the deep-set eyes hope flits
As he the back unto the burden fits.
Within this rugged man of brains and brawn
The quiv'ring nation's high powered currents drawn,
As waves of love and kindness he transmits.

O prairie poet, prophet, children's friend!
Great-brained, great-willed, great-hearted man and
    true,
May we, like thee, in prayerful patience plod
With courage toward the wished for, peaceful end!
May we thy helpful friendliness renew,
Thou war worn soul communing with thy God!

Charlotte B. Jordan

Included by permission of the Sun.

TO THE MEMORY OF ABRAHAM
LINCOLN
(1865)

O, slow to smite and swift to spare,
    Gentle and merciful and just!
Who, in the fear of God, didst bear
    The sword of power—a nation's trust.

In sorrow by thy bier we stand,
    Amid the awe that hushes all,
And speak the anguish of a land
    That shook with horror at thy fall.

Thy task is done—the bond are free;
    We bear thee to an honored grave,
Whose noblest monument shall be
    The broken fetters of the slave.

Pure was thy life; its bloody close
    Hath placed thee with the sons of light,
Among the noble host of those
    Who perished in the cause of right.

William Cullen Bryant

*From the "Collected Works" of William Cullen Bryant.
Included by permission of D. Appleton & Company.*

TOLLING
(April 15, 1865)

Tolling, tolling, tolling!
    All the bells of the land!
Lo, the patriot martyr
    Taketh his journey grand!
Travels into the ages,
    Bearing a hope how dear!
Into life's unknown vistas,
    Liberty's great pioneer.

Tolling, tolling, tolling!
    See, they come as a cloud,
Hearts of a mighty people,
    Bearing his pall and shroud.
Lifting up, like a banner,
    Signals of loss and woe;
Wonder of breathless nations,
    Moveth a solemn show.

Tolling, tolling, tolling!
    Was it, O man beloved,
Was it thy funeral only
    Over the land that moved?

Veiled by that hour of anguish,
    Borne into the rebel rout,
Forth into utter darkness,
    Slavery's curse went out.

Lucy Larcom

Included by permission of Houghton Mifflin Company.

TWO HEROES
(*From the "Columbian Ode"*)

When foolish kings, at odds with swift-paced Time,
    Would strike that banner down,
A nobler knight than ever writ or rhyme
Has starred with fame's bright crown
Through armed hosts bore it free to float on high
Beyond the clouds, a light that cannot die.
    Ah, hero of our younger race,
    Strong builder of a temple new,
    Ruler who sought no lordly place,
    Warrior who sheathed the sword he drew!—
    Lover of men, who saw afar
    A world unmarred by want or war,
    Who knew the path, and yet forbore
    To tread till all men should implore;
    Who saw the light, and led the way
    Where the grey world might greet the day;
    Father and leader, prophet sure,
    Whose will in vast works shall endure,

How shall we praise him on this day of days,
Great son of fame who has no need of praise?

How shall we praise him? Open wide the doors
Of the fair temple whose broad base he laid.
Through its white halls a shadowy cavalcade
Of heroes moves on unresounding floors—
Men whose brawned arms upraised these columns high,
And reared the towers that vanish in the sky—
The strong who, having wrought, can never die.

And here, leading a gallant host, comes one
Who held a warring nation in his heart;
Who knew love's agony, but had no part
In love's delight; whose mighty task was done
Through blood and tears that we might walk in joy,
And this day's rapture feel no sad alloy.
Around him heirs of bliss, whose bright brows wear
Palm-leaves amid their laurels ever fair.

Gaily they come, as though the drum
Beat out the call their glad hearts knew so well;
Brothers once more, dear as of yore,
Who in a noble conflict nobly fell.
Their blood washed pure yon banner in the sky,
And quenched the brands under these arches high—
The brave who, having fought, can never die.

Harriet Monroe

Revised by the author.
Included by permission of the author and The Macmillan Company.

YOUNG LINCOLN

Men saw no portents on that night
A hundred years ago. No omens flared
Above that rail-built cabin with one door,
And windowless to all the peering stars.
They laid him in the hollow of a log,
Humblest of cradles, save that other one—
The manger in the stall at Bethlehem.

No portents! yet with whisper and alarm
The Evil Powers that dread the nearing feet
Of heroes held a council in that hour;
And sent three fates to darken that low door
To baffle and beat back the heaven-sent child.
Three were the fates—gaunt Poverty that chains,
Gray Drudgery that grinds the hope away,
And gaping Ignorance that starves the soul.

They came with secret laughters to destroy.
Ever they dogged him, counting every step,
Waylaid his youth and struggled for his life.
They came to master, but he made them serve.
And from the wrestle with the destinies,
He rose with all his energies aglow.

45

For God, upon whose steadfast shoulders rest
These governments of ours, had not forgot.
He needed for His purposes a voice,
A voice to be a clarion on the wind,
Crying the word of freedom to dead hearts,
The word the centuries had waited for.

So hidden in the West, God shaped His man.
There in the unspoiled solitudes he grew,
Unwarped by culture and uncramped by creed;
Keeping his course courageous and alone,
As goes the Mississippi to the sea.
His daring spirit burst the narrow bounds,
Rose resolute; and like the sea-called stream,
He tore new channels where he found no way.

The tools were his first teachers, sternly kind.
The plow, the scythe, the maul, the echoing axe,
Taught him their homely wisdom and their peace
He had the plain man's genius—common sense,
Yet rage for knowledge drove his mind afar;
He fed his spirit with the bread of books,
And slaked his thirst at all the wells of thought.

But most he read the heart of common man,
Scanned all its secret pages stained with tears,
Saw all the guile, saw all the piteous pain;

46

ABRAHAM LINCOLN

And yet could keep the smile about his lips,
Love and forgive, see all and pardon all;
His only fault, the fault that some of old
Laid even on God—that he was ever wont
To bend the law to let his mercy out.

Edwin Markham

Revised by the author.
Included by permission of the author.

George Washington In Poetry

Soldier and statesman, rarest unison;
High-poised example of great duties done
Simply as breathing, a world's honors worn
As life's indifferent gifts to all men born.

James Russell Lowell

GEORGE WASHINGTON

AT THE TOMB OF WASHINGTON

Here let the brows be bared
  Before the land's great son,
He who undaunted dared,
  Our Washington!

From dole, despair and doubt,
  Deceit and enmity,
He led us up and out
  To Victory.

A Pharos in the night,
  A pillar in the dawn,
By his inspiring light
  May we fare on!

Day upon hastening day
  Still let us reverence him;
Fame, never, never may
  His laurels dim!

Clinton Scollard

Included by permission of the author

EPITAPH ON WASHINGTON

The defender of his country,—the founder of
liberty,
History and tradition are explored in vain
For a parallel to his character.
In the annals of modern greatness
He stands alone;
And the noblest names of antiquity
Lose their lustre in his presence.
Born the benefactor of mankind,
He united all the greatness necessary
To an illustrious career.
Nature made him great,
He made himself virtuous.
Called by his Country to the defense of her
liberties,
He triumphantly vindicated the rights of humanity,
And, on the pillars of National Independence
Laid the foundation of a great Republic.

Twice invested with Supreme Magistracy
By the unanimous vote of a free people,
He surpassed, in the Cabinet,
The glories of the field,

GEORGE   WASHINGTON

And, voluntarily resigning the scepter and the
sword,
Retired to the shades of private life;
A spectacle so new, and so sublime,
Was contemplated with profoundest admiration
And the name of Washington,
Adding new lustre to humanity,
Resounded to the remotest regions of the earth.
Magnanimous in youth,
Glorious through life,
Great in death;
His highest ambition, the happiness of mankind;
His noblest victory, the conquest of himself,
Bequeathing to posterity the inheritance of his fame.
And building his monument in the hearts of his
Countrymen,—
He lived—the ornament of the Eighteenth Cen-
tury;
He died, regretted by a mourning world.

Anonymous

GEORGE   WASHINGTON

Only a baby, fair and small,
  Like many another baby son,
Whose smiles and tears come swift at call;
Who ate, and slept, and grew, that's all—
  The infant Washington.

53

Only a boy, like other boys,
    With tasks and studies, sports and fun;
Fond of his books and games and toys;
Living his childish griefs and joys—
    The little Washington.

Only a lad, awkward and shy,
    Skilled in handling a horse or gun;
Mastering knowledge that, by and by,
Should aid him in duties great and high—
    The youthful Washington.

Only a man of finest bent,
    Hero of battles fought and won;
Surveyor, General, President,
Who served his country, and dies content—
    The patriot Washington.

Only—ah! what was the secret, then,
    Of his being America's honored son?
Why was he famed above other men?
His name upon every tongue and pen—
    The illustrious Washington.

A mighty brain, a will to endure,
    Passions subdued, a slave to none,
A heart that was brave and strong and sure,

GEORGE   WASHINGTON

A soul that was noble and great and pure,
A faith in God that was held secure—
　This was George Washington.

　　　　　　　　　　Anonymous

GEORGE   WASHINGTON

This was the man God gave us when the hour
Proclaimed the dawn of Liberty begun;
Who dared a deed, and died when it was done,
Patient in triumph, temperate in power,—
Not striving like the Corsican to tower
To heaven, nor like great Philip's greater son.
To win the world and weep for worlds unwon,
Or lose the star to revel in the flower.
The lives that serve the eternal verities
Alone do mould mankind, Pleasure and pride
Sparkle awhile and perish, as the spray
Smoking across the crests of the cavernous seas
Is impotent to hasten or delay
The everlasting surges of the tide.

　　　　　　　　　　John Hall Ingham

INSCRIPTION AT MOUNT VERNON

Washington, the brave, the wise, the good.
Supreme in war, in council, and in peace.
Valiant without ambition, discreet without fear,
        confident without presumption.
In disaster calm; in success, moderate; in all, himself.
The hero, the patriot, the Christian.
The father of nations, the friend of mankind,
Who, when he had won all, renounced all, and sought
    in the bosom of his family and of nature,
    retirement, and in the hope of religion,
    immortality.

Anonymous

A MAN!

About his brow the laurel and the bay
    Was often wreathed,—on this our memory
    dwells,—
Upon whose bier in reverence today
    We lay these immortelles.

His was a vital, virile, warrior soul;
    If force were needed, he exalted force;
Unswerving as the pole star to the pole,
    He held his righteous course.

GEORGE   WASHINGTON

He smote at Wrong, if he believed it Wrong,
　　As did the Knight, with stainless accolade;
He stood for Right, unfalteringly strong,
　　Forever unafraid.

With somewhat of the savant and the sage,
　　He was, when all is said and sung, a man,
The flower imperishable of this valient age,—
　　A true American!

Clinton Scollard

Included by permission of the author and The Sun.

MOUNT VERNON, THE HOME OF
WASHINGTON

There dwelt the Man, the flower of human kind,
Whose visage mild bespoke his nobler mind.

There dwelt the Soldier, who his sword ne'er drew
But in a righteous cause, to Freedom true.

There dwelt the Hero, who ne'er killed for fame,
Yet gained more glory than a Caesar's name.

There dwelt the Statesman, who, devoid of art,
Gave soundest counsels from an upright heart;

And, O Columbia, by thy sons caressed,
There dwelt the Father of the realms he blessed;

Who no wish felt to make his mighty praise,
Like other chiefs, the means himself to raise;

But there retiring, breathed in pure renown,
And felt a grandeur that disdained a crown.

William Day

OLD SONG WRITTEN DURING WASHINGTON'S LIFE

Americans, rejoice;
While songs employ the voice,
    Let trumpets sound.
The thirteen stripes display
In flags and streamers gay,
'Tis Washington's birthday,
    Let joy abound.

Long may he live to see
This land of liberty
    Flourish in peace;
Long may he live to prove
A grateful people's love,
And late to heaven remove,
    Where joys ne'er cease.

GEORGE WASHINGTON

Fill the glass to the brink,
Washington's health we'll drink,
   'Tis his birthday.
Glorious deeds he has done,
By him our cause is won,
Long live great Washington!
    Huzza! Huzza!

Anonymous

THE SHIP OF STATE

Thou, too, sail on, O Ship of State!
Sail on, O Union, strong and great!
Humanity with all its fears,
With all the hopes of future years,
Is hanging breathless on thy fate!
We know what master laid thy keel,
What Workmen wrought thy ribs of steel,
Who made each mast, and sail, and rope,
What anvils rang, what hammers beat,
In what a forge and what a heat
Were shaped the anchors of thy hope!
Fear not each sudden sound and shock,
'Tis of the wave and not the rock;
'Tis but the flapping of the sail,
And not a rent made by the gale!

59

In spite of rock and tempest's roar,
In spite of false lights on the shore,
Sail on, nor fear to breast the sea!
Our hearts, our hopes, our prayers, our tears,
Our faith triumphant o'er our fears,
Are all with thee,—are all with thee!

Henry Wadsworth Longfellow

Included by permission of Houghton, Mifflin Company.

TRIBUTE TO WASHINGTON

Great without pomp, without ambition brave,
Proud, not to conquer fellow-men, but save;
Friend to the weak, a foe to none but those
Who plan their greatness on their brethren's woes;
Aw'd by no titles—undefil'd by lust—
Free without faction—obstinately just;
Warm'd by religion's sacred, genuine ray,
That points to future bliss the unerring way;
Yet ne'er control'd by superstition's laws,
That worst of tyrants in the noblest cause.

From a London Newspaper

TWO HEROES
(From the "Columbian Ode")

When foolish kings, at odds with swift-paced Time,
        Would strike that banner down,
A nobler knight than ever writ or rhyme
Has starred with fame's bright crown
Through armed hosts bore it free to float on high
Beyond the clouds, a light that cannot die.
        Ah, hero of our younger race,
        Strong builder of a temple new,
        Ruler who sought no lordly place,
        Warrior who sheathed the sword he drew!—
        Lover of men, who saw afar
        A world unmarred by want or war,
        Who knew the path, and yet forbore
        To tread till all men should implore;
        Who saw the light, and led the way
        Where the grey world might greet the day;
        Father and leader, prophet sure,
        Whose will in vast works shall endure.
How shall we praise him on this day of days,
Great son of fame who has no need of praise?

How shall we praise him?   Open wide the doors
Of the fair temple whose broad base he laid.

Through its white halls a shadowy cavalcade
Of heroes moves on unresounding floors—
Men whose brawned arms upraised these columns high,
And reared the towers that vanish in the sky—
The strong who, having wrought, can never die.

And here, leading a gallant host, comes one
Who held a warring nation in his heart;
Who knew love's agony, but had no part
In love's delight; whose mighty task was done
Through blood and tears that we might walk in joy,
And this day's rapture feel no sad alloy.
Around him heirs of bliss, whose bright brows wear
Palm-leaves amid their laurels ever fair.
Gaily they come, as though the drum
Beat out the call their glad hearts knew so well;
Brothers once more, dear as of yore,
Who in a noble conflict nobly fell.
Their blood washed pure yon banner in the sky,
And quenched the brands under these arches high—
The brave who, having fought, can never die.

Harriet Monroe

Revised by the author.
Included by permission of the author and The Macmillan Company.

GEORGE WASHINGTON

UNION AND LIBERTY

Flag of the heroes who left us their glory,
 Borne through their battle-fields' thunder and flame,
Blazoned in song and illumined in story,
 Wave o'er us all, who inherit their fame!
  Up with our banner bright,
  Sprinkled with starry light,
 Spread its fair emblems from mountain to shore,
  While through the sounding sky
  Loud rings the Nation's cry,—
UNION AND LIBERTY! ONE EVERMORE!

Light of our firmament, guide of our Nation,
 Pride of her children, honored afar,
Let the wide beams of thy full constellation
 Scatter each cloud that would darken a star!
  Up with our banner bright,
  Sprinkled with starry light,
 Spread its fair emblems from mountain to shore,
  While through the sounding sky
  Loud rings the Nation's cry,—
UNION AND LIBERTY! ONE EVERMORE!

Empire unsceptred! what foe shall assail thee,
 Bearing the standard of Liberty's van?

Think not the God of thy fathers shall fail thee,
   Striving with men for the birthright of man!
      Up with our banner bright,
      Sprinkled with starry light,
   Spread its fair emblems from mountain to shore.
      While through the sounding sky
      Loud rings the Nation's cry,—
UNION AND LIBERTY! ONE EVERMORE!

Yet, if by madness and treachery blighted,
   Dawns the dark hour when the sword thou must
         draw,
Then with the arms of thy million united,
   Smite the bold traitors to Freedom and Law!
      Up with our banner bright,
      Sprinkled with starry light,
   Spread its fair emblems from mountain to shore,
      While through the sounding sky
      Loud rings the Nation's cry,—
UNION AND LIBERTY! ONE EVERMORE!

Lord of the Universe! shield us and guide us,
   Trusting Thee always, through shadow and sun!
Thou hast united us, who shall divide us?
   Keep us, oh keep us the MANY IN ONE!
      Up with our banner bright,
      Sprinkled with starry light,

GEORGE WASHINGTON

Spread its fair emblems from mountain to shore,
   While through the sounding sky,
   Loud rings the Nation's cry,—
UNION AND LIBERTY! ONE EVERMORE!

Oliver Wendell Holmes

Included by permission of Houghton Mifflin Company.

WASHINGTON

Where may the wearied eye repose
   When gazing on the Great;
Where neither guilty glory glows,
   Nor despicable state?
Yes—one—the first—the last—the best—
The Cincinnatus of the West,
   Whom envy dare not hate,
Bequeath the name of Washington,
To make men blush there was but one!

Lord Byron

WASHINGTON

Soldier and statesman, rarest unison;
High-poised example of great duties done
Simply as breathing, a world's honors worn
As life's indifferent gifts to all men born;

Dumb for himself, unless it were to God,
But for his barefoot soldiers eloquent,
Tramping the snow to corral where they trod,
Held by his awe in hollow-eyed content;
Modest, yet firm as Nature's self; unblamed
Save by the men his nobler temper shamed;
Never seduced through show of present good
By other than unsetting lights to steer
New-trimmed in Heaven, nor than his steadfast mood
More steadfast, far from rashness as from fear;
Rigid, but with himself first, grasping still
In swerveless poise the wave-beat helm of will;
Not honored then or now because he wooed
The popular voice, but that he still withstood;
Broad-minded, higher-souled, there is but one
Who was all this and ours, and all men's,—Washington.

James Russell Lowell
(*From "Under the Elm"*)

Included by permission of Houghton Mifflin Company.

WASHINGTON

It seems so simple now, that life of thine,
To us who from these turgid days look back,
As mariners from 'neath a stormy wrack
Peer out and see a verdant island shine

GEORGE WASHINGTON

Behind them, where the storm has left no sign
Save freshness and new glory in its track;
To us, who midst sunk rocks still turn and tack,
So seem thy days all happy, free and fine.

Yet, wert thou here, wouldst not thy piercing gaze,
Thy steady hand and strong, compelling will,
Unravel the mixt strands of good and ill
That so perplex?   In youth through wildwood maze
Thy skill surveyed clear paths; and later, lo!
The way was straight because thou mad'st it so.

Geraldine Meyrich

Included by permission of Overland Monthly.

WASHINGTON

Thou gallant Chief whose glorious name
Doth still adorn the Book of Fame:
Whose deeds shall live while freemen prize
The cause for which the Patriot dies,
Long to Columbia may'st thou be
The beacon light of Liberty.

Rev. Denis O'Crowley

WASHINGTON

Our Nation's birth gave history your name,
  Recording on its pages your great deeds.
No hesitation marred when duty came,
  No clouds obscured from you your country's needs.
Pure were the thoughts you planted in man's heart,
  Nor is your harvest fully garnered yet;
Still grows and thrives the tree that had its start,
  In hallowed ground with honest purpose wet.
Each passing day your wisdom is revealed,
  Each added year some richer promise gives;
Your presence led our fathers in the field,
  Your spirit leads us still to that which lives
In Liberty and Peace, for which you fought
  To gain Eternity, the goal you sought.

John A. Prentice

Included by permission of Overland Monthly.

WASHINGTON

O noble brow, so wise in thought!
O heart, so true! O soul unbought!
O eye, so keen to pierce the night
And guide the "ship of state" aright!
O life so simple, grand and free,
The humblest still may turn to thee.
O king, uncrowned! O prince of men!

GEORGE   WASHINGTON

When shall we see thy like again?
The century, just passed away,
Has felt the impress of thy sway,
While youthful hearts have stronger grown
And made thy patriot zeal their own.
In marble hall or lowly cot,
Thy name hath never been forgot.
The world itself is richer, far,
For the clear shining of a star.
And loyal hearts in years to run
Shall turn to thee, O Washington.

Mary Wingate

WASHINGTON MONUMENT BY NIGHT

1

The stone goes straight.
A lean swimmer dives into night sky,
Into half-moon mist.

2

Two trees are coal black.
This is a great white ghost between.
It is cool to look at.
Strong men, strong women, come here.

3

Eight years is a long time
To be fighting all the time.

4

The republic is a dream.
Nothing happens unless first a dream.

5

The wind bit hard at Valley Forge one Christmas.
Soldiers tied rags on their feet.
Red footprints wrote on the snow.   .   .
.   .   .   and stone shoots into stars here
.   .   .   into half-moon mist to-night.

6

Tongues wrangled dark at a man.
He buttoned his overcoat and stood alone.
In a snowstorm, red hollyberries, thoughts,
      he stood alone.

7

Women said: He is lonely
.   .   .   fighting   .   .   .   fighting   .   .   .   eight
      years.   .   .

8

The name of an iron man goes over the world.
It takes a long time to forget an iron man.

9

.   .   .   .
.   .   .   .

Carl Sandburg

From "Slabs of the Sunburnt West."
Included by permission of the author and Harcourt, Brace and Company.

GEORGE WASHINGTON

WASHINGTON'S BIRTHDAY

All honor to that day which long ago
    Gave birth to him who Freedom's cause espoused;
Who, by his ardor in the sacred fight,
    The fire and strength of patriots aroused;
Who knew no master, save that One divine
    Whose strength was his, who knew no fear, save
        one—
The fear of doing wrong! All hail the day
    That gave to Freedom's cause George Washington.

Years come and go, and generations fall
    Into the dust. The world its heroes gives.
They step upon the stage, then pass away
    And are no more, but Freedom ever lives.
And while it lives, and while its banner bright
    Is upward flung into the golden sun,
Within the heart of every freeman's child
    Will live that honored name, George Washington.

Then honor to the day that gave him birth,
    For it is also Freedom's natal day.
Let all who worship Freedom's cause stand forth
    And to his memory their homage pay.
And let each loyal son the work take up—
    For, know ye, Freedom's work is never done—
And greater, grander, build the edifice
    Begun so long ago by Washington.

Arthur J. Burdick

71

WASHINGTON'S MONUMENT

For him who sought his country's good
In plains of war, 'mid scenes of blood;
Spent the warm noon of life's bright day,
Who in the dubious battle's fray,
That to a world he might secure
Rights that forever shall endure,
      Rear the monument of fame!
      Deathless is the hero's name.

For him, who, when the war was done,
And victory sure, and freedom won,
Left glory's theatre, the field,
The olive branch of peace to wield;
And proved, when at the helm of state,
Though great in war, in peace as great;
      Rear the monument of fame!
      Deathless is the hero's name!

For him, whose worth, though unexpress'd,
Lives cherished in each freeman's breast,
Whose name, to patriot souls so dear,
Time's latest children shall revere,
Whose brave achievements praised shall be,
While beats one breast for liberty;
      Rear the monument of fame!
      Deathless is the hero's name!

GEORGE   WASHINGTON

But why for him vain marbles raise?
Can the cold sculpture speak his praise?
Illustrious shade! we can proclaim
Our gratitude, but not thy fame.
Long as Columbia shall be free,
She lives a monument of thee,
     And may she ever rise in fame,
     To honor thy immortal name!

Anonymous

WASHINGTON'S   TOMB

Would we could coin for thee new words of praise;
To call thee only great, is meaningless;
Thou didst the woes of humankind redress,
And the blest standard of our freedom raise;
Didst lead us safe o'er strange, untrodden ways,
And in thy life—that did all truth express—
Teach us thy cherished creed which we confess,
The equal rights of men to crown their days.
Thou didst not sleep in sound of city's toil;
The din of traffic, murmur of the mart,
Are far away; within thy native soil
We leave thee, heart of honor, Honor's heart;
Not in cathedral's gorgeous sculptured gloom,
But 'neath thy much loved stars, a fitter tomb.

Ruth Lawrence

From "Colonial Verses" by Ruth Lawrence.
Included by permission of the author and Brentano's.

WASHINGTON'S VOW

How felt the land in every part
The strong throb of a nation's heart?
As its great leader gave, with reverent awe,
His pledge to Union, Liberty, and Law!

That pledge the heavens above him heard,
That vow the sleep of centuries stirred.
In world-wide wonder listening peoples bent
Their gaze on Freedom's great experiment.

. . . . .

Thank God! the people's choice was just!
The one man equal to his trust.
Wise without lore, and without weakness good,
Calm in the strength of flawless rectitude.

. . . . .

Our first and best—his ashes lie
Beneath his own Virginia sky.
Forgive, forget, oh! true and just and brave,
The storm that swept above thy sacred grave.

. . . . .

Then let the sovereign millions where
Our banner floats in sun and air,
From the warm palm-lands to Alaska's cold,
Repeat with us the pledge, a century old!

John Greenleaf Whittier

YOUNG WASHINGTON
(The Embassy to the French Forts, 1753)

Tie the moccasin, bind the pack,
Sling your rifle across your back,
Up! and follow the mountain track,
    Tread the Indian Trail.
North and west is the road we fare
Toward the forts of the Frenchmen, where
"Peace or War!" is the word we bear,
    Life and Death in the scale.

The leaves of October are dry on the ground,
The sheaves of Virginia are gathered and bound,
Her fallows are glad with the cry of the hound,
    The partridges whirr in the fern;
But deep are the forests and keen are the foes
Where Monongahela in wilderness flows;
We've labors and perils and torrents and snows
    To conquer before we return.

Hall and council-room, farm and chase,
Coat of scarlet and frill of lace
All are excellent things in place;
    Joy in these if ye can.
Mine be hunting-shirt, knife and gun,

75

OUR HOLIDAYS IN POETRY

Camp aglow on the sheltered run,
Friend and foe in the checkered sun;
That's the life for a man!

Arthur Guiterman

Revised by the author.
From "I Sing the Pioneer," copyright 1926, by E. P. Dutton & Company. Included by permission of the author.

EASTER IN POETRY

In every trembling bud and bloom
    That cleaves the earth, a flowery sword,
I see Thee come from out the tomb,
    Thou risen Lord.

.   .   .   .

Thou art not dead! Thou art the whole
    Of life that quickens in the sod;
Green April is Thy very soul,
    Thou great Lord God.

Charles Hanson Towne

EASTER

AFRAID?

Afraid? Of whom am I afraid?
Not death; for who is he?
The porter of my father's lodge
As much abasheth me.

Of life? 'Twere odd I fear a thing
That comprehendeth me
In one or more existences
At Deity's decree.

Of resurrection? Is the east
Afraid to trust the morn
With her fastidious forehead?
As soon impeach my crown!

Emily Dickinson

ALL THINGS BRIGHT AND BEAUTIFUL

All things bright and beautiful,
All creatures great and small,
All things wise and wonderful,
The Lord God made them all.

79

Each little flower that opens,
    Each little bird that sings,
He made their glowing colours,
    He made their tiny wings.

The rich man in his castle,
    The poor man at his gate,
God made them, high or lowly,
    And order'd their estate.

The purple-headed mountain,
    The river running by,
The sunset and the morning,
    That brightens up the sky;—

The cold wind in the winter,
    The pleasant summer sun,
The ripe fruits in the garden,—
    He made them every one.

The tall trees in the greenwood,
    The meadows where we play,
The rushes by the water
    We gather every day;—

He gave us eyes to see them,
    And lips that we might tell,
How great is God Almighty,
    Who has made all things well.

Cecil Frances Alexander

APRIL AND MAY

April cold with dropping rain
Willows and lilacs brings again,
The whistle of returning birds,
And the trumpet-lowing of the herds.
The scarlet maple-keys betray
What potent blood hath modest May,
What fiery force the earth renews,
The wealth of forms, the flush of hues;
What joy in rosy waves outpoured
Flows from the heart of Love, the Lord.

Ralph Waldo Emerson

AT EASTER TIME

The little flowers came through the ground,
    At Easter time, at Easter time;
They raised their heads and looked around,
    At happy Easter time.
And every pretty bud did say,
    "Good people, bless this holy day,
For Christ is risen, the angels say
    At happy Easter time!"

The pure white lily raised its cup
    At Easter time, at Easter time;
The crocus to the sky looked up
    At happy Easter time.
"We'll hear the song of Heaven!" they say,
    "Its glory shines on us today.
Oh! may it shine on us always
    At holy Easter time!"

'Twas long and long and long ago,
    That Easter time, that Easter time;
But still the pure white lilies blow
    At happy Easter time.
And still each little flower doth say,
    "Good Christians, bless this holy day,
For Christ is risen, the angels say
    At blessed Easter time!"

Laura E. Richards

Included by permission of the author.

THE AWAKENING

    You little, eager, peeping thing—
    You embryonic point of light
    Pushing from out your winter night,
    How you do make my pulses sing!
    A tiny eye amid the gloom—

EASTER

The merest speck I scarce had seen—
So doth God's rapture rend the tomb
In this wee burst of April green!

And lo, 'tis here!—and lo, 'tis there!—
Spurting its jets of sweet desire
In upward curling threads of fire
Like tapers kindling all the air.
Why, scarce it seems an hour ago
These branches clashed in bitter cold;
What Power hath set their veins aglow?
O soul of mine, be bold, be bold!
If from this tree, this blackened thing,
Hard as the floor my feet have prest,
This flame of joy comes clamoring
In hues as red as robin's breast
Waking to life this little twig—
O faith of mine, be big! be big!

Angela Morgan

Included by permission of the author.

BUTTERCUPS AND DAISIES

Buttercups and daisies,
    Oh, the pretty flowers!
Coming, ere the spring-time,
    To tell of sunny hours.

While the trees are leafless,
  While the fields are bare,
Buttercups and daisies
  Spring up everywhere.

Ere the snow-drop peepeth,
  Ere the crocus bold,
Ere the early primrose
  Opes its paly gold,
Somewhere on a sunny bank
  Buttercups are bright,
Somewhere 'mong the frozen grass
  Peeps the daisy white.

Little hardy flowers,
  Like to children poor,
Playing in their sturdy health
  By their mother's door,
Purple with the north wind,
  Yet alert and bold,
Fearing not, and caring not,
  Though they be a-cold.

What to them is weather?
  What are stormy showers?
Buttercups and daisies
  Are these human flowers!

EASTER

He who gave them hardship
    And a life of care,
Gave them likewise hardy strength
    And patient hearts to bear.

Welcome, yellow buttercups!
    Welcome, daisies white!
Ye are in my spirit
    Visioned, a delight!
Coming ere the spring-time,
    Of sunny hours to tell,
Speaking to our hearts of Him
    Who doeth all things well.

Mary Howitt

EASTER

Sky where the white clouds stand in prayer,
    Luminous, lucent Easter sky!
Easter fields with their vivid flare
    Of wind-tossed blossoms that die
Only to blossom again some day!
Make us remember we're that way,
Brave little blossoms, sweet and gay!
Make us remember we shall, too,
Know, as you know the sun and dew

Over again—know all the sweet
Of being alive again, and meet
As you meet the friendly blossoms near,
Those who to us were near and dear.

Sky, with your Easter white and blue,
    Teach us, like you, to pray!
Blossoms of Easter, make us, too,
    As brave as you and as gay!

Mary Carolyn Davies

Included by permission of the author.

EASTER

I got me flowers to strew Thy way,
I got me boughs off many a tree.
But Thou wast up at break of day
And broughtst Thy sweets along with Thee.

The Sun arising in the East,
Though he give light and th' East perfume,
If they should offer to contest
With Thy arising, they presume.

EASTER

Can there be any day but this,
Though many suns to shine endeavor?
We count three hundred, but we miss:
There is but one, and that one ever.

George Herbert

EASTER

Once more the Ancient Wonder
    Brings back the goose and crane
Prophetic Sons of Thunder,
    Apostles of the Rain.

In many a battling river
    The broken gorges boom.
Behold the Mighty Giver
    Emerges from the Tomb!

Now robins chant the story
    Of how the wintery sward
Is litten with the glory
    Of the Angel of the Lord.

His countenance is lightening,
    And still his robe is snow,
As when the dawn was brightening
    Two thousand years ago.

O who can be a stranger
        To what has come to pass?
The Pity of the Manger
        Is mighty in the grass!

Undaunted by Decembers,
        The sap is faithful yet,
The giving Earth remembers
        And only men forget!

John G. Neihardt

Included by permission of the author and The Macmillan Company.

EASTER

The barrier stone has rolled away,
        And loud the angels sing;
The Christ comes forth this blessed day
        To reign, a deathless king.
For shall we not believe He lives
        Through such awakening?
Behold, how God each April gives
        The miracle of Spring.

Edwin L. Sabin

AN EASTER CANTICLE

In every trembling bud and bloom
    That cleaves the earth, a flowery sword,
I see Thee come from out the tomb,
    Thou risen Lord.

In every April wind that sings
    Down lanes that make the heart rejoice
Yea, in the word the wood-thrush brings,
    I hear Thy voice.

Lo! every tulip is a cup
    To hold Thy morning's brimming wine
Drink, O my soul, the wonder up—
    Is it not Thine?

The great Lord God, invisible,
    Hath roused to rapture the green grass;
Through sunlit mead and dew-drenched dell,—
    I see Him pass.

His old immortal glory wakes
    The rushing streams and emerald hills;
His ancient trumpet softly shakes
    The daffodils.

Thou art not dead! Thou art the whole
    Of life that quickens in the sod;
Green April is Thy very soul,
    Thou great Lord God.

Charles Hanson Towne

ncluded by permission of the author.

EASTER CAROL

O Earth! throughout thy borders
    Re-don thy fairest dress;
And everywhere, O Nature!
    Throb with new happiness;
Once more to new creation
    Awake, and death gainsay,
For death is swallowed up of life,
    And Christ is risen to-day!

Let peals of jubilation
    Ring out in all the lands;
With hearts of deep elation
    Let sea with sea clasp hands;
Let one supreme Te Deum
    Roll round the World's highway,
For death is swallowed up of life,
    And Christ is risen to-day!

George Newell Lovejoy

From *The Chautauquan, April* 1902.
Included by permission of the Chautauqua Press.

AN EASTER CAROL

Spring bursts to-day,
  For Christ is risen and all the earth's at play.

    Flash forth, thou Sun,
The rain is over and gone, its work is done.
    Winter is past,
Sweet Spring is come at last, is come at last.
    Bud, Fig and Vine,
Bud, Olive, fat with fruit and oil and wine.
    Break forth this morn
In roses, thou but yesterday a Thorn.
    Uplift thy head,
O pure white Lily through the Winter dead.
    Beside your dams
Leap and rejoice, you merry-making Lambs.
    All Herds and Flocks
Rejoice, all Beasts of thickets and of rocks.
    Sing, Creatures, sing,
Angels and Men and Birds and everything.
    All notes of Doves
Fill all our world: this is the time of loves.

Christina G. Rossetti

From "Poems" by Christina Rossetti.
Included by permission of The Macmillan Company.

AN EASTER HYMN

Spake the Lord Christ—"I will arise:"
    It seemed a saying void and vain—
    How shall a dead man rise again?—
Vain as our tears, vain as our cries;
    Not one of all the little band
    That loved Him this might understand.

"I will arise," Lord Jesus said—
    Hearken, amid the morning dew,
    Mary, a voice that calleth you!
Then Mary turned her golden head,
    And lo! there shining at her side
    Her Master they had crucified.

At dawn, to his dim sepulchre,
    Mary, remembering that far day,
    When at his feet the spikenard lay,
Came, bringing balm and spice and myrrh;
    To her the grave had made reply:
    "He is not here—He cannot die."

Praetor and priest in vain conspire,
    Jerusalem and Rome in vain
    Torture the god with mortal pain,
To quench that seed of living fire;
    But light that had in heaven its birth
    Can never be put out on earth.

EASTER

"I will arise"—across the years,
     Even as to Mary that grey morn,
     To us that gentle voice is born:
"I will arise."—He that hath ears
     O ponder well this mystic word;
     Let not the Master speak unheard.

No soul descended deep in hell,
     The child of sorrow, sin and death,
     The Immortal Spirit suffereth
To see corruption; though it fell
     From loftiest station in the skies,
     It still to heaven again must arise.

No dream of faith, no seed of love,
     No lonely action nobly done,
     But is as stable as the sun,
And fed and watered from above;
     From nether base to starry cope
     Nature's two laws are Faith and Hope.

Safe in the care of heavenly powers,
     The good we dreamed but might not do,
     Lost beauty, magically new,
Shall spring as surely as the flowers,
     When, mid the sobbing of the rain,
     The heart of April beats again.

Celestial spirit that doth roll
    The heart's sepulchral stone away,
    Be this our resurrection day,
The singing Easter of the soul—
    O gentle Master of the Wise,
    Teach us to say: "I will arise."

Richard Le Gallienne

Published by permission of the author and The Woman's Home Companion.

EASTER HYMN

Christ the Lord is risen to-day,
Sons of men and angels say:
Raise your joys and triumphs high,
Sing, ye heavens, and earth reply.

Love's redeeming work is done,
Fought the fight, the battle won;
Lo! our Sun's eclipse is o'er;
Lo! He sets in blood no more.

Vain the stone, the watch, the seal;
Christ hath burst the gates of hell!
Death in vain forbids His rise;
Christ hath opened Paradise!

EASTER

Lives again our glorious King:
Where, O Death, is now thy sting?
Once He died, our souls to save:
Where thy victory, O Grave?

Charles Wesley

EASTER MORNING

Most glorious Lord of life, that on this day
    Didst make thy triumph over death and sin,
    And, having harrowed hell, didst bring away
Captivity thence captive, us to win;
This joyous day, dear Lord, with joy begin,
And grant that we, for whom thou didst die,
Being with Thy dear blood clean washed from sin,
May live forever in felicity:
And that Thy love we weighing worthily
May likewise love Thee for the same again:
And for Thy sake, that all like dear didst buy,
With love may one another entertain.
So let us love, dear Love, like as we ought;
Love is the lesson which the Lord us taught.

Edmund Spenser

EASTER NIGHT

All night had shout of men and cry
    Of woeful women filled His way;
Until that noon of sombre sky
    On Friday, clamour and display
Smote Him; no solitude had He,
No silence, since Gethsemane.

Public was Death; but Power, but Might,
    But Life again, but Victory,
Were hushed within the dead of night,
    The shutter'd dark, the secrecy.
And all alone, alone, alone
He rose again behind the stone.

Alice Meynell

Included by permission of Wilfrid Meynell.

EASTER SONG

Snowdrops, lift your timid heads,
    All the earth is waking,
Field and forest, brown and dead,
    Into life are waking;
Snowdrops, rise and tell the story
    How He rose, the Lord of glory.

96

EASTER

Lilies! lilies! Easter calls,
    Rise to meet the dawning
Of the blessed light that falls
    Thro' the Easter morning;
Ring your bells and tell the story,
    How He rose, the Lord of glory.

Waken, sleeping butterflies,
    Burst your narrow prison;
Spread your golden wings and rise,
    For the Lord is risen;
Spread your wings and tell the story,
    How He rose, the Lord of glory.

Mary A. Lathbury

EASTER WEEK

See the land, her Easter keeping,
    Rises as her Maker rose.
Seeds, so long in darkness sleeping,
    Burst at last from winter snows.
Earth with heaven above rejoices,
    Fields and gardens hail the spring;
Shaughs and woodlands ring with voices,
    While the wild birds build and sing.

You to whom your Maker granted
 Powers to those sweet birds unknown,
Use the craft by God implanted;
 Use the reason not your own.
Here, while heaven and earth rejoices,
 Each his Easter tribute bring—
Work of fingers, chant of voices,
 Like the birds who build and sing.

Charles Kingsley

THE ELIXIR

Teach me, my God and King,
 In all things Thee to see,
And what I do in anything,
 To do it as for Thee.

All may of Thee partake:
 Nothing can be so mean
Which with this tincture, for Thy sake,
 Will not grow bright and clean.

A servant with this clause
 Makes drudgery divine;
Who sweeps a room as for Thy laws,
 Makes that and the action fine.

EASTER

This is the famous stone
    That turneth all to gold;
For that which God doth touch and own
    Cannot for less be told.

George Herbert

FAITH

In every leaf that crowns the plain,
In every violet 'neath the hill,
In every yellow daffodil. . . .
I see the risen Lord again!

In each arbutus flower I see
A faith that lived through frost and snow,
And in the birds that northward go,
A guiding hand's revealed to me.

Lo! winter from some dark abyss
Came forth to kill all growing things:
'Twas vain, spring rose on emerald wings,
Mothlike from her dead chrysalis.

Each germ within the tiny seed
Throws off the husk that to it clings,
And towards the sun it upward brings
New life to blossom to its need.

Ye hearts that mourn rise up and sing!
Death has no power to hold his prey,
The grave is only where we lay
The soul, for its eternal spring! . . .

In every leaf that crowns the plain,
In every violet 'neath the hill,
In every yellow daffodil.   .   .   .
I see the risen Lord again!

John Richard Moreland

Included by permission of the author.

THE GLORY OF GOD IN CREATION

Thou art, O God, the life and light
    Of all this wondrous world we see;
Its glow by day, its smile by night,
    Are but reflections caught from Thee.
Where'er we turn, Thy glories shine,
And all things fair and bright are Thine.

When day, with farewell beam, delays
    Among the opening clouds of even,
And we can almost think we gaze
    Through opening vistas into heaven,
Those hues that make the sun's decline
So soft, so radiant, Lord, are Thine.

EASTER

When night, with wings of starry gloom,
   O'ershadows all the earth and skies,
Like some dark, beauteous bird, whose plume
   Is sparkling with unnumbered eyes,
That sacred gloom, those fires divine,
So grand, so countless, Lord, are Thine.

When youthful Spring around us breathes,
   Thy spirit warms her fragrant sigh,
And every flower that Summer wreathes
   Is born beneath Thy kindling eye:
Where'er we turn, Thy glories shine,
And all things fair and bright are Thine.

Thomas Moore

GOD, WHO HATH MADE THE DAISIES

God, who hath made the daisies
   And ev'ry lovely thing,
He will accept our praises,
   And hearken while we sing.
He says though we are simple,
   Though ignorant we be,
"Suffer the little children,
   And let them come to Me."

Though we are young and simple,
  In praise we may be bold;
The children in the temple
  He heard in days of old.
And if our hearts are humble,
  He says to you and me,
"Suffer the little children,
  And let them come to Me."

He sees the bird that wingeth
  Its way o'er earth and sky;
He hears the lark that singeth
  Up in the heaven high;
But sees the hearts' low breathings,
  And says (well pleased to see),
"Suffer the little children,
  And let them come to Me."

Therefore we will come near Him,
  And solemnly we'll sing;
No cause to shrink or fear Him,
  We'll make our voices ring;
For in our temple speaking,
  He says to you and me,
"Suffer the little children,
  And let them come to Me."

E. P. Hood

HOLY, HOLY, HOLY

Holy, holy, holy, Lord God Almighty!
    Early in the morning our songs shall rise to Thee;
Holy, holy, holy! merciful and mighty!
    God in Three Persons, Blessed Trinity!

Holy, holy, holy! all the saints adore Thee,
    Casting down their golden crowns around the
        glassy sea,
Cherubim and seraphim falling down before Thee,
    Who wert and art, and evermore shalt be!

Holy, holy, holy! though the darkness hide Thee,
    Though the eye of sinful man Thy glory may not
        see,
Only Thou art holy, there is none beside Thee,
    Perfect in power, in love, in purity!

Holy, holy, holy, Lord God Almighty!
    All Thy works shall praise Thy name in earth and
        sky and sea;
Holy, holy, holy! merciful and mighty!
    God in Three Persons, Blessed Trinity.

Reginald Heber

HYMN TO THE CREATION

The spacious firmament on high,
With all the blue ethereal sky,
And spangled heaven, a shining frame,
Their great original proclaim;
Th' unwearied sun, from day to day,
Does his Creator's power display,
And publishes to every land
The work of an Almighty hand.

Soon as the evening shades prevail,
The moon takes up the wond'rous tale,
And nightly to the list'ning earth
Repeats the story of her birth;
Whilst all the stars that round her burn,
And all the planets in their turn,
Confirm the tidings as they roll,
And spread the news from pole to pole.

What though, in solemn silence, all
Move round the dark, terrestrial ball?
What though no real voice nor sound
Amid their radiant orbs be found?
In reason's ear they all rejoice,
And utter forth a glorious voice,
Forever singing as they shine,
"The hand that made us is divine."

Joseph Addison

JOY, SHIPMATE, JOY!

Joy, shipmate, joy!
(Pleased to my soul at death I cry)
Our life is closed, our life begins,
The long, long anchorage we leave,
The ship is clear at last, she leaps!
She swiftly courses from the shore,
Joy, shipmate, joy!

Walt Whitman

Included by permission of Doubleday, Page & Co.

KING ROBERT OF SICILY

Robert of Sicily, brother of Pope Urbane
And Valmond, Emperor of Allemaine,
Appareled in magnificent attire
With retinue of many a knight and squire,
On St. John's eve, at vespers, proudly sat
And heard the priests chant the Magnificat.
And as he listened, o'er and o'er again
Repeated, like a burden or refrain,
He caught the words, "Deposuit potentes
 De sede, et exaltavit humiles";
And slowly lifting up his kingly head,
He to a learned clerk beside him said,

105

"What mean these words?"   The clerk made answer
                                meet,
"He has put down the mighty from their seat,
And has exalted them of low degree."
Thereat King Robert muttered scornfully,
" 'Tis well that such seditious words are sung
Only by priests, and in the Latin tongue;
For unto priests, and people be it known,
There is no power can push me from my throne,"
And leaning back he yawned and fell asleep,
Lulled by the chant monotonous and deep.

When he awoke, it was already night;
The church was empty, and there was no light,
Save where the lamps, that glimmered few and faint,
Lighted a little space before some saint.
He started from his seat and gazed around,
But saw no living thing and heard no sound.
He groped towards the door, but it was locked;
He cried aloud, and listened, and then knocked,
And uttered awful threatenings and complaints,
And imprecations upon men and saints.
The sounds re-echoed from the roof and walls
As if dead priests were laughing in their stalls.

At length the sexton, hearing from without
The tumult of the knocking and the shout,
And thinking thieves were in the house of prayer,

106

Came with his lantern, asking, "Who is there?"
Half choked with rage, King Robert fiercely said,
"Open; 'tis I, the King! Art thou afraid?"
The frightened sexton, muttering, with a curse,
"This is some drunken vagabond, or worse!"
Turned the great key and flung the portal wide;
A man rushed by him at a single stride,
Haggard, half-naked, without hat or cloak,
Who neither turned, nor looked at him, nor spoke,
But leaped into the blackness of the night,
And vanished like a spectre from his sight.

Robert of Sicily, brother of Pope Urbane
And Valmond, Emperor of Allemaine,
Despoiled of his magnificient attire,
Bare-headed, breathless, and besprent with mire,
With sense of wrong and outrage desperate,
Strode on and thundered at the palace gate;
Rushed through the court-yard, thrusting in his rage
To right and left each seneschal and page,
And hurried up the broad and sounding stair,
His white face ghastly in the torches' glare.
From hall to hall he passed with breathless speed;
Voices and cries he heard, but did not heed,
Until at last he reached the banquet-room,
Blazing with light, and breathing with perfume.

There on the dais sat another king,
Wearing his robes, his crown, his signet ring—
King Robert's self in features, form, and height,
But all transfigured with angelic light!
It was an Angel; and his presence there
With a divine effulgence filled the air,
An exaltation, piercing the disguise,
Though none the hidden Angel recognize.

A moment speechless, motionless, amazed,
The throneless monarch on the Angel gazed,
Who met his look of anger and surprise
With the divine compassion of his eyes!
Then said, "Who art thou, and why com'st thou
    here?"
To which King Robert answered with a sneer,
"I am the King, and come to claim my own
From an imposter, who usurps my throne!"
And suddenly, at these audacious words,
Up sprang the angry guests, and drew their swords;
The Angel answered, with unruffled brow,
"Nay, not the King, but the King's Jester; thou
Henceforth shalt wear the bells and scalloped cape,
And for thy counselor shalt lead an ape;
Thou shalt obey my servants when they call,
And wait upon my henchmen in the hall!"

Deaf to King Robert's threats and cries and prayers,
They thrust him from the hall and down the stairs;

EASTER

A group of tittering pages ran before,
And they opened wide the folding door,
His heart failed, for he heard, with strange alarms,
The boisterous laughter of the men-at-arms,
And all the vaulted chamber roar and ring
With the mock plaudits of "Long live the King!"
Next morning, waking with the day's first beam,
He said within himself, "It was a dream!"
But the straw rustled as he turned his head;
There were the cap and bells beside his bed;
Around him rose the bare, discolored walls,
Close by, the steeds were champing in their stalls,
And in the corner, a revolting shape,
Shivering and chattering, sat the wretched ape.
It was no dream; the world he loved so much
Had turned to dust and ashes at his touch!

Days came and went; and now returned again
To Sicily the old Saturnian reign;
Under the Angel's governance benign
The happy island danced with corn and wine,
And deep within the mountain's burning breast
Enceladus, the giant, was at rest.

Meanwhile King Robert yielded to his fate,
Sullen and silent and disconsolate.
Dressed in the motley garb that Jesters wear,
With look bewildered, and a vacant stare,

Close shaven above the ears, as monks are shorn,
By courtiers mocked, by pages laughed to scorn,
His only friend the ape, his only food
What others left—he still was unsubdued,
And when the Angel met him on his way,
And half in earnest, half in jest, would say,
Sternly, though tenderly, that he might feel
The velvet scabbard held a sword of steel,
"Art thou the King?" the passion of his woe
Burst from him in resistless overflow,
And lifting high his forehead, he would fling
The haughty answer back, "I am, I am the King!"

Almost three years were ended, when there came
Ambassadors of great repute and name
From Valmond, Emperor of Allemaine,
Unto King Robert, saying that Pope Urbane
By letter summoned them forthwith to come
On Holy Thursday to his city of Rome.
The Angel with great joy received his guests,
And gave them presents of embroidered vests,
And velvet mantles with rich ermine lined,
And rings and jewels of the rarest kind.
Then he departed with them o'er the sea
Into the lovely land of Italy,
   Whose loveliness was more resplendent made
   By the mere passing of that cavalcade

With plumes, and cloaks, and housings, and the stir
Of jeweled bridle and of golden spur.

And lo! among the menials, in mock state,
Upon a piebald steed, with shambling gait,
His cloak of foxtails flapping in the wind,
The solemn ape demurely perched behind,
King Robert rode, making huge merriment
In all the country towns through which they went.

The Pope received them with great pomp, and blare
Of bannered trumpets, on St. Peter's square,
Giving his benediction and embrace,
Fervent, and full of apostolic grace.
While with congratulations and with prayers
He entertained the Angel unawares,
Robert, the Jester, bursting through the crowd,
Into their presence rushed, and cried aloud:
"I am the King! Look and behold in me
Robert, your brother, King of Sicily!
This man, who wears my semblance to your eyes,
Is an impostor in a king's disguise.
Do you not know me? Does no voice within
Answer my cry, and say we are akin?"
The Pope in silence, but with troubled mien,
Gazed at the Angel's countenance serene;
The Emperor, laughing, said, "It is strange sport
To keep a madman for thy Fool at court!"

And the poor, baffled Jester, in disgrace
Was hustled back among the populace.

In solemn state the Holy Week went by,
And Easter Sunday gleamed upon the sky;
The presence of the Angel, with its light,
Before the sun rose, made the city bright,
And with new fervor filled the hearts of men,
Who felt that Christ indeed had risen again.
Even the Jester, on his bed of straw,
With haggard eyes the unwonted splendor saw;
He felt within a power unfelt before,
And kneeling humbly on his chamber floor,
He heard the rushing garments of the Lord
Sweep through the silent air, ascending heavenward.

And now the visit ending, and once more
Valmond returning to the Danube's shore,
Homeward the Angel journeyed, and again
The land was made resplendent with his train,
Flashing along the towns of Italy
Unto Salerno, and from thence by sea.
And when once more within Palermo's wall,
And, seated on the throne in his great hall,
He heard the Angelus from convent towers,
As if the better world conversed with ours,
He beckoned to King Robert to draw nigher,
And with a gesture bade the rest retire,

EASTER

And when they were alone, the Angel said
"Art thou the King?" Then, bowing down his head,
King Robert crossed both hands upon his breast,
And meekly answered him, "Thou knowest best!
My sins as scarlet are; let me go hence,
And in some cloister's school of penitence,
Across those stones that pave the way to heaven,
Walk barefoot, till my guilty soul be shriven!"

The Angel smiled, and from his radiant face
A holy light illumined all the place,
And through the open window, loud and clear,
They heard the monks chant in the chapel near,
Above the stir and tumult of the street,
"He has put down the mighty from their seat,
And has exalted them of low degree!"
And through the chant a second melody
Rose like the throbbing of a single string:
"I am an Angel, and thou art the King!"

King Robert, who was standing near the throne,
Lifted his eyes, and lo! he was alone!
But all appareled as in days of old,
With ermined mantle and with cloth of gold;
And when his courtiers came they found him there,
Kneeling upon the floor, absorbed in silent prayer.

Henry Wadsworth Longfellow

Included by permission of Houghton Mifflin Company.

THE LAST VIOLET

The gray old Owl could scarce believe his eyes,
The Squirrel dropped a chestnut in surprise,
The Raven croaked, the Bullfrog stared outright,
The Bunny blinked to see so strange a sight.

A Violet, loveliest of Flowerkind,
Shivering and shaking in the autumn wind.
Her head was bowed; faintly they heard her cry,
"Oh, why has Summer left me here to die?"

"You happy birds! The Dear God gave you wings
To follow Summer in her wanderings,
While I who came too late to see her face
Shall soon be turned to dust and leave no trace!

"And yet deep in my root this thought I keep,
That Winter may be nothing but a Sleep.
If it be true God marks a petal's fall,
How can it be that winter ends it all?

"The Caterpillar told me a strange thing,
How that he dreamed about a Future Spring
When 'neath a sapphire sky, through scented bowers
He'll flutter on bright wings 'mid rainbow flowers."

114

EASTER

The Raven cawed, "Oh, Violet, if I
Were you I wouldn't tell the Butterfly.
I really think the blow would almost kill her.
To be descended from a Caterpillar!"

The Squirrel flicked his tail and arched his back;
Here was a nut too hard for him to crack.
"Good-by, my dear, if I don't stir about,
I sha'n't have nuts to last the winter out."

The Gray Owl shook his head. "I know more things
My dear, than any bird that flies on wings,
But there are wonders in the sea and land
Even the wisest Owl can't understand."

A silence fell. 'Twas broken by the Frog:
"I am descended from a Polliwog,
About the lowest thing in Nature's scale,
An armless, legless creature *with a tail!*

"Yet who in beauty with a Frog can vie?
And Beauty, we are told, can never die.
You, too, have Beauty, so sleep well, my dear,
And happy dreams, we'll meet again next year!"

Oliver Herford

Included by permission of the author and the Curtis Publishing Company.

THE LENT LILY

'Tis spring; come out to ramble
   The hilly brakes around,
For under thorn and bramble
   About the hollow ground
   The primroses are found.

And there's the windflower chilly
   With all the winds at play,
And there's the Lenten lily
   That has not long to stay
   And dies on Easter day.

And since till girls go maying
   You find the primrose still,
And find the windflower playing
   With every wind at will,
   But not the daffodil.

Bring baskets now, and sally
   Upon the spring's array,
And bear from hill and valley
   The daffodil away
   That dies on Easter day.

A. E. Housman

Included by permission of the author.

LOVELIEST OF TREES

Loveliest of trees, the cherry now
Is hung with bloom along the bough,
And stands about the woodland ride
Wearing white for Eastertide.

Now, of my threescore years and ten,
Twenty will not come again,
And take from seventy springs a score,
It only leaves me fifty more.

And since to look at things in bloom
Fifty springs are little room,
About the woodlands I will go
To see the cherry hung with snow.

A. E. Housman

Included by permission of the author.

THE MAJESTY AND MERCY OF GOD

Oh, worship the King all glorious above;
Oh, gratefully sing His power and His love;
Our shield and defender, the Ancient of Days
Pavilioned in splendor and girded with praise.

Oh, tell of His might, Oh, sing of His grace,
Whose robe is the light, whose canopy space;
His chariots of wrath the deep thunder clouds form,
And dark is His path on the wings of the storm.

The earth, with its store of wonders untold,
Almighty, Thy power hath founded of old,
Hath established it fast by a changeless decree,
And round it hath cast, like a mantle, the sea.

Thy bountiful care what tongue can recite?
It breathes in the air, it shines in the light,
It streams from the hills, it descends to the plain,
And sweetly distills in the dew and the rain.

Frail children of dust and feeble as frail
In thee do we trust, nor find thee to fail.
Thy mercies how tender, how firm to the end,
Our Maker, Defender, Redeemer and Friend.

Oh, measureless Might, ineffable Love,
While angels delight to hymn Thee above,
The humbler creation, though feeble their lays,
With true adoration shall lisp to Thy praise.

Sir Robert Grant

118

MAY IS BUILDING HER HOUSE

May is building her house.   With apple blooms
She is roofing over the glimmering rooms:
Of the oak and the beech hath she builded its beams,
And, spinning all day at her secret looms,
With arras of leaves each wind-swayed wall
She pictureth over, and peopleth it all
  With echoes and dreams,
  And singing of streams.

May is building her house of petal and blade:
Of the roots of the oak is the flooring made,
  With a carpet of mosses and lichen and clover,
  Each small miracle over and over,
And tender, travelling green things strayed.

Her windows the morning and evening star,
And her rustling doorways, ever ajar
  With the coming and going
  Of fair things blowing,
The thresholds of the four winds are.

May is building her house.   From the dust of things
She is making the songs and the flowers and the wings:
  From October's tossed and trodden gold
  She is making the young year out of the old:

119

Yea! out of winter's flying sleet
She is making all the summer sweet,
  And the brown leaves spurned of November's feet
She is changing back again to spring's.

Richard Le Gallienne

Included by permission of the author.

THE MIRACLE

Yesterday the twig was brown and bare;
Today the glint of green is there;
Tomorrow will be leaflets spare;
I know no thing so wondrous fair,
No miracle so strangely rare.

I wonder what will next be there!

L. H. Bailey

Included by permission of the author.

NATURE'S CREED

I believe in the brook as it wanders
    From hillside into glade;
I believe in the breeze as it whispers
    When evening's shadows fade.

120

EASTER

I believe in the roar of the river
  As it dashes from high cascade;
I believe in the cry of the tempest
  'Mid the thunder's cannonade.
I believe in the light of shining stars,
  I believe in the sun and the moon;
I believe in the flash of lightning,
  I believe in the night-bird's croon.
I believe in the faith of the flowers,
  I believe in the rock and sod,
For in all of these appeareth clear
  The handiwork of God.

Anonymous

NATURE'S EASTER MUSIC

The flowers from the earth have arisen,
  They are singing their Easter-song;
Up the valleys and over the hillsides
  They come, an unnumbered throng.

Oh, listen! The wild flowers are singing
  Their beautiful song without words!
They are pouring the soul of their music
  Through the voices of happy birds.

Every flower to a bird has confided
    The joy of its blossoming birth—
The wonders of its resurrection
    From its grave, the frozen earth.

For you, chirp the wren and the sparrow,
    Little Eyebright, Anemone pale!
Gay Columbine, orioles are chanting
    Your trumpet-note, loud on the gale.

The Buttercup's thanks for the sunshine
    The gold finch's twitter reveals;
And the Violet trills, through the bluebird,
    Of the heaven that within her she feels.

The song-sparrow's exquisite warble
    Is born in the heart of the Rose—
Of the wild-rose, shut in its calyx,
    Afraid of belated snows.

And the melody of the wood-thrush
    Floats up from the nameless and shy
White blossoms that stay in the cloister
    Of pine-forests, dim and high.

The dust of the roadside is vocal:
    There is music from every clod;
Bird and breeze are the wild-flowers' angels,
    Their messages bearing to God.

EASTER

"We arise and we praise Him together!"
  With a flutter of petals and wings,
The anthem of spirits immortal
  Rings back from created things.

And nothing is left wholly speechless:
  For the dumbest life that we know
May utter itself through another,
  And double its gladness so.

Lucy Larcom

From "Poems" by Lucy Larcom.
Included by permission of Houghton Mifflin Company.

ON A GLOOMY EASTER

I hear the robins singing in the rain.
  The longed-for Spring is hushed so drearily
  That hungry lips cry often wearily,
"Oh, if the blessed sun would shine again!"

I hear the robins singing in the rain.
  The misty world lies waiting for the dawn;
  The wind sobs at my window and is gone,
And in the silence come old throbs of pain.

But still the robins sing on in the rain,
  Not waiting for the morning sun to break,
  Nor listening for the violets to wake,
Nor fearing lest the snow may fall again.

My heart sings with the robins in the rain,
    For I remember it is Easter morn,
    And life and love and peace are all new born,
And joy has triumphed over loss and pain.

Sing on, brave robins, sing on in the rain!
    You know behind the clouds the sun must shine,
    You know that death means only life divine
And all our losses turn to heavenly gain.

I lie and listen to you in the rain.
    Better than Easter bells that do not cease,
    Your message from the heart of God's great peace,
And to his arms I turn and sleep again.

Alice Freeman Palmer

Included by permission of George H. Palmer.

PIPPA'S SONG

The year's at the spring
And day's at the morn;
Morning's at seven;
The hillside's dew-pearled;
The lark's on the wing;
The snail's on the thorn;
God's in His heaven—
All's right with the world!

Robert Browning

PROVIDENCE

Lo, the lilies of the field,
How their leaves instruction yield!
Hark to Nature's lesson given
By the blessed birds of heaven!
Every bush and tufted tree
Warbles sweet philosophy:
Mortal, fly from doubt and sorrow;
God provideth for the morrow.

Say, with richer crimson glows
The kingly mantle than the rose?
Say, have kings more wholesome fare
Than we citizens of air?
Barns nor hoarded grain have we,
Yet we carol merrily.
Mortal, fly from doubt and sorrow;
God provideth for the morrow.

One there lives, whose guardian eye
Guides our humble destiny;
One there lives, who, Lord of all,
Keeps our feathers lest they fall.

Pass we blithely then the time,
Fearless of the snare and lime,
Free from doubt and faithless sorrow:
God provideth for the morrow.

Reginald Heber

PSALM XXIII

The Lord is my shepherd;
I shall not want.

He maketh me to lie down in green pastures:
He leadeth me beside still waters.
He restoreth my soul:
He guideth me in paths of righteousness for his
name's sake.

Yea, though I walk through the valley of the
shadow of death
I will fear no evil;
For Thou art with me:
Thy rod and Thy staff, they comfort me:

Thou preparest a table before me
In the presence of mine enemies:
Thou anointest my head with oil:
My cup runneth over.

EASTER

Surely goodness and mercy shall follow me all the
days of my life:
And I will dwell in the house of the Lord forever.

The Bible

PSALM CIV—*Selected*

Bless the Lord, O my soul.
    O Lord my God, Thou art very great;
Thou art clothed with honour and majesty:
    Who coverest Thyself with light as with a garment;
Who stretchest out the heavens like a curtain;
    Who layeth the beams of His chambers in the
        waters;
Who maketh the clouds His chariot;
    Who walketh upon the wings of the wind;
Who maketh winds His messengers;
    His ministers a flaming fire.

Who laid the foundations of the earth,
    That it should not be moved forever,
Thou coverest it with the deep as with a vesture;
    The waters stood above the mountains.
At Thy rebuke they fled;
    At the voice of Thy thunder they hasted away;
They went up by the mountains, they went down
        by the valleys,
    Unto the place which Thou hadst founded for
        them.

Thou hast set a bound that they may not pass over;
    That they turn not again to cover the earth.

He sendeth forth springs into the valleys;
    They run among the mountains:
They give drink to every beast of the field;
    The wild asses quench their thirst.
By them the fowl of heaven have their habitation,
    They sing among the branches.
He watereth the mountains from His chambers:
    The earth is satisfied with the fruit of Thy works.
He causeth the grass to grow for the cattle,
    And herb for the service of man.

O Lord, how manifold are Thy works!
In wisdom hast Thou made them all.

The Bible

SOFTLY THROUGH THE MELLOW STARLIGHT

Softly through the mellow starlight
    Steals a strain of silver song:
Lo the echoing hills proclaim it,
    Waft the glad refrain a-long.
Glory, glory, Christ is risen!
    Whispered in the star-lit way,

128

EASTER

List the lovely shades re-echo
    Christ the Lord is ris'n to-day.

Happy bands in shining raiment
    Fill the arch of Heaven's dome,
Sweep their harps to strains so tender
    Wafted from their distant home.
                                    Glory, etc.

Softly through life's shaded valley
    Comes once more the silver strain,
Borne on angel pinions to us,
    And we join the sweet refrain.
                                    Glory, etc.

From Carols Old and Carols New.
Copyrighted, 1905 by Charles L. Hutchins.

THE SONG OF THE LILIES

The lilies say on Easter day,
    "We give, we give,
We breathe our fragrance on the air,
We shed our beauty everywhere!
    We give, we give."

The lilies say on Easter day,
    "We live, we live.

In darkness buried long we lay;
The sun awoke us one spring day!
    We live, we live."

The lilies say on Easter day,
    "Give, children, give!
Give love and kindness everywhere;
They truly live who truly share!
    Give, children, give."

Lucy Wheelock

Included by permission of the author.

A SONG OF WAKING

The maple buds are red, are red,
    The robin's call is sweet;
The blue sky floats above thy head,
    The violets kiss thy feet.
The sun paints emeralds on the spray,
    And sapphires on the lake;
A million wings unfold to-day.
    A million flowers awake.

Their starry cups the cowslips lift
    To catch the golden light,
And like a spirit fresh from shrift
    The cherry tree is white.

EASTER

The innocent looks up with eyes
    That know no deeper shade
Than falls from wings of butterflies
    Too fair to make afraid.

With long green raiment blown and wet,
    The willows hand in hand
Lean low to teach the rivulet
    What trees may understand
Of murmurous tune and idle dance,
    With broken rhymes whose flow
A poet's ear will catch, perchance,
    A score of miles below.

Across the sky to fairy realm
    There sails a cloud-born ship;
A wind sprite standeth at the helm,
    With laughter on his lip;
The melting masts are tipped with gold,
    The 'broidered pennons stream;
The vessel beareth in her hold
    The lading of a dream.

It is the hour to rend thy chains,
    The blossom time of souls;
Yield all the rest to cares and pains,
    To-day delight controls.

Gird on thy glory and thy pride,
    For growth is of the sun;
Expand thy wings whate'er betide,
    The Summer is begun.

Katharine Lee Bates

Included by permission of the author.

TALKING IN THEIR SLEEP

    "You think I am dead,"
    The apple-tree said,
"Because I have never a leaf to show—
    Because I stoop,
    And my branches droop,
And the dull gray mosses over me grow!
But I'm alive in trunk and shoot;
    The buds of next May
    I fold away—
But I pity the withered grass at my foot."

    "You think I am dead,"
    The quick grass said,
"Because I have parted with stem and blade!
    But under the ground
    I am safe and sound,
With the snow's thick blanket over me laid.

EASTER

I'm all alive, and ready to shoot
    Should the spring of the year
    Come dancing here—
But I pity the flower without branch or root."

"You think I am dead,"
    A soft voice said,
"Because not a branch or root I own!
    I never have died,
    But close I hide
In a plumy seed that the wind has sown.
Patient I wait through the long winter hours;
    You will see me again—
    I shall laugh at you then,
Out of the eyes of a hundred flowers!"

Edith M. Thomas

Included by permission of Houghton Mifflin Company.

A TRUE LENT

Is this a fast, to keep
    The larder lean,
    And clean
From fats of veals and sheep?

Is it to quit the dish
    Of flesh, yet still
      To fill
The platter high with fish?

Is it to fast an hour,
    Or ragg'd to go,
      Or show
A downcast look and sour?

No: 'tis a fast to dole
    Thy sheaf of wheat
      And meat
Unto the hungry soul.

It is to fast from strife,
    From old debate
      And hate;
To circumcise thy life.

To show a heart grief-rent;
    To starve thy sin,
      Not bin:
And that's to keep thy Lent.

Robert Herrick

134

'TWAS AT THE MATIN HOUR

'Twas at the matin hour,
    Before the early dawn;
The prison doors flew open,
    The bolts of death were drawn.

'Twas at the matin hour,
    When pray'rs of saints are strong;
When two short days ago
    He bore the spitting, wounds and wrong.

From realms unseen, an unseen way,
    Th' Almighty Saviour came,
And following on His silent steps,
    An angel armed in flame.

The stone is rolled away,
    The keepers fainting fall,
Satan and Pilate's watchmen,
    The day has scared them all.

The angel came full early,
    But Christ had gone before,
Not for Himself, but for his Saints,
    Is burst the prison door.

When all His Saints assemble,
    Make haste ere twilight cease,
His Easter blessing to receive,
    And so lie down in peace.

Fourteenth Century Carol

Included by permission of Gordon Hutchins.

UNDER THE LEAVES

Oft have I walked these woodland paths,
    Without the blessed foreknowing
That underneath the withered leaves
    The fairest buds were growing.

Today the south-wind sweeps away
    The types of autumn's splendor,
And shows the sweet arbutus flowers,—
    Spring's children, pure and tender.

O prophet-flowers!—with lips of bloom,
    Outvying in your beauty
The pearly tints of ocean shells,—
    Ye teach me faith and duty!

Walk life's dark ways, ye seem to say,
    With love's divine foreknowing
That where man sees but withered leaves,
    God sees sweet flowers growing.

Albert Laighton

THE WAKING YEAR

A lady red upon the hill
    Her annual secret keeps;
A lady white within the field
    In placid lily sleeps!

The tidy breezes with their brooms
    Sweep vale, and hill, and tree;
Prithee, my pretty housewives,
    Who may expected be?

The neighbors do not yet suspect,
    The woods exchange a smile—
Orchard, and buttercup, and bird—
    In such a little while!

And yet how still the landscape stands,
    How nonchalant the wood,
As if the resurrection
    Were nothing very odd!

Emily Dickinson

YE HEAVENS, UPLIFT YOUR VOICE

Ye heav'ns uplift your voice;
    Sun, moon, and stars, rejoice;
And thou, too, nether earth,
    Join in the common mirth:
For winter storm at last,
    And rain is over-past:
Instead whereof the green
    And fruitful palm is seen.

Ye flow'rs of Spring, appear;
    Your gentle heads uprear,
And let the growing seed
    Enamel lawn and mead.
Ye roses inter-set
    With clumps of violet,
Ye lilies white, unfold
    In beds of marigold.

Ye birds with open throat
    Prolong your sweetest note;
Awake, ye blissful quires,
    And strike your merry lyres:

EASTER

For why? unhurt by Death,
  The Lord of life and breath,
Jesus, as He foresaid,
  Is risen from the dead.

     Fifteenth Century Carol

Included by permission of Gordon Hutchins.

ARBOR DAY IN POETRY

What does he plant who plants a tree?
He plants the friend of sun and sky;
He plants the flag of breezes free;
The shaft of beauty, towering high;
He plants a home to heaven anigh
    For song and mother-croon of bird
    In hushed and happy twilight heard—
The treble of heaven's harmony—
These things he plants who plants a tree.

Henry Cuyler Bunner

ARBOR DAY

A B C'S IN GREEN

The trees are God's great alphabet:
With them He writes in shining green
Across the world His thoughts serene.
He scribbles poems against the sky
With a gay, leafy lettering,
For us and for our bettering.

The wind pulls softly at His page,
And every star and bird
Repeats in dutiful delight His word,
And every blade of grass
Flutters to class.

Like a slow child that does not heed,
I stand at summer's knees,
And from the primer of the wood
I spell that life and love are good,
I learn to read.

Leonora Speyer

Included by permission of the author.

APPLE-SEED JOHN

Poor Johnny was bended well nigh double
With years of toil, and care, and trouble;
But his large old heart still felt the need
Of doing for others some kindly deed.

"But what can I do?" old Johnny said:
"I who work so hard for daily bread?
It takes heaps of money to do much good;
I am far too poor to do as I would."

The old man sat thinking deeply a while,
Then over his features gleamed a smile,
And he clapped his hands with a boyish glee,
And said to himself: "There's a way for me!"

He worked, and he worked with might and main,
But no one knew the plan in his brain.
He took ripe apples in pay for chores,
And carefully cut from them all the cores.

He filled a bag full, then wandered away,
And no man saw him for many a day.
With knapsack over his shoulder slung,
He marched along, and whistled or sung.

ARBOR DAY

He seemed to roam with no object in view,
Like one who had nothing on earth to do;
But, journeying thus o'er the prairies wide,
He paused now and then, and his bag untied.

With pointed cane deep holes he would bore,
And in every hole he placed a core;
Then covered them well, and left them there
In keeping of sunshine, rain and air.

Sometimes for days he waded through grass,
And saw not a living creature pass,
But often, when sinking to sleep in the dark,
He heard the owls hoot and the prairie-dogs bark.

Sometimes an Indian of sturdy limb
Came striding along and walked with him;
And he who had food shared with the other,
As if he had met a hungry brother.

When the Indian saw how the bag was filled,
And looked at the holes that the white man drilled.
He thought to himself 'twas a silly plan
To be planting seed for some future man.

Sometimes a log cabin came in view,
Where Johnny was sure to find jobs to do,
By which he gained stores of bread and meat,
And welcome rest for his weary feet.

He had full many a story to tell,
And goodly hymns that he sung right well;
He tossed up the babes, and joined the boys
In many a game full of fun and noise.

And he seemed so hearty, in work or play,
Men, women and boys all urged him to stay;
But he always said: "I have something to do
And I must go on to carry it through."

The boys, who were sure to follow him round,
Soon found what it was he put in the ground;
And so, as time passed and he traveled on,
Ev'ry one called him "Old Apple-Seed John."

Whenever he'd used the whole of his store,
He went into cities and worked for more;
Then he marched back to the wilds again,
And planted seed on hill-side and plain.

In cities, some said the old man was crazy;
While others said he was only lazy;
But he took no notice of gibes and jeers,
He knew he was working for future years.

He knew that trees would soon abound
Where once a tree could not have been found;
That a flick'ring play of light and shade
Would dance and glimmer along the glade;

146

ARBOR DAY

That blossoming sprays would form fair bowers,
And sprinkle the grass with rosy showers;
And the little seeds his hands had spread,
Would become ripe apples when he was dead.

So he kept on traveling far and wide,
Till his old limbs failed him, and he died.
He said at the last: " 'Tis a comfort to feel
I've done good in the world, though not a great deal."

Weary travelers, journeying west,
In the shade of his trees find pleasant rest;
And they often start, with glad surprise,
At the rosy fruit that round them lies.

And if they inquire whence came such trees,
Where not a bough once swayed in the breeze,
The answer still comes, as they travel on:
"Those trees were planted by Apple-Seed John."

Lydia Maria Child

AN ARBOR DAY TREE

Dear little tree that we plant to-day,
What will you be when we're old and gray?
"The savings bank of the squirrel and mouse,
For robin and wren an apartment house,

The dressing-room of the butterfly's ball,
The locust's and katydid's concert hall,
The schoolboy's ladder in pleasant June,
The schoolgirl's tent in the July noon,
And my leaves shall whisper them merrily
A tale of the children who planted me."

Anonymous

BE DEFERENT TO TREES

The talking oak
To the ancients spoke.

But any tree
Will talk to me.

What truths I know
I garnered so.

But those who want to talk and tell,
    And those who will not listeners be,
Will never hear a syllable
    From out the lips of any tree.

Mary Carolyn Davies

Included by permission of the author.

148

ARBOR   DAY

BEATUS VIR

Happy is the man who loves the woods and waters,
    Brother to the grass, and well-beloved of Pan;
The earth shall be his, and all her laughing daughters
    Happy the man.

Never grows he old, nor shall he taste of sorrow,
    Happy at the day's end as when the day began,
Yesterday forgotten, unshadowed by To-morrow,—
    Happy the man.

Followed by the mountains, ne'er his heart is lonely,
    Talked to all day by rivers as they run,
The earth is his love, as he who loves one only—
    Happy the man.

His gossips are the stars, and the moon-rise his tavern
    He who seeks a better, find it if he can—
And O his sweet pillow in the ferny cavern!
    Happy the man.

Richard Le Gallienne

Included by permission of the author.

BIRCH TREES

The night is white,
    The moon is high,
The birch trees lean
    Against the sky.

The cruel winds
    Have blown away
Each little leaf
    Of silver gray.

O lonely trees
    As white as wool—
That moonlight makes
    So beautiful.

John Richard Moreland

*From The Personalist, University of Southern California.
Included by permission of the author.*

CHILD'S SONG IN SPRING

The silver birch is a dainty lady,
    She wears a satin gown;
The elm-tree makes the old church-yard shady,
    She will not live in town.

ARBOR DAY

The English oak is a sturdy fellow,
    He gets his green coat late;
The willow is smart in a suit of yellow,
    While brown the beech-trees wait.

Such a gay green gown God gives the larches—
    As green as He is good!
The hazels hold up their arms for arches
    When Spring rides through the wood.

The chestnut's proud and the lilac's pretty,
    The poplar's gentle and tall,
But the plane-tree's kind to the poor dull city—
    I love him best of all!

E. Nesbit

Included by permission of the author.

DAPHNE

Do you not hear her song
When rosy showers fall
And forest whispers call
    Along?

Do you not hear her feet
Now faint among the leaves—
Or is't the wind that grieves
    So sweet?

Do you her face not see
'Mid laurels of a glade
Where sunbeams pass—half maid
    Half tree?

                  Thomas S. Jones, Jr.

Included by permission of the author.

FAMILY TREES

You boast about your ancient line,
But listen, stranger, unto mine:

You trace your lineage afar,
Back to the heroes of a war
Fought that a country might be free;
Yea, farther—to a stormy sea
Where winter's angry billows tossed,
O'er which your Pilgrim Fathers crossed.
Nay, more—through yellow, dusty tomes
You trace your name to English homes
Before the distant, unknown West
Lay open to a world's behest;
Yea, back to days of those Crusades
When Turk and Christian crossed their blades,
You point with pride to ancient names,

152

ARBOR DAY

To powdered sires and painted dames;
You boast of this—your family tree;
Now listen, stranger, unto me:

When armored knights and gallant squires,
Your own beloved, honored sires,
Were in their infants' blankets rolled,
My fathers' youngest sons were old;
When they broke forth in infant tears
My fathers' heads were crowned with years,
Yea, ere the mighty Saxon host,
Of which you sing, had touched the coast,
Looked back as far as you look now,
Yea, when the Druids trod the wood,
My venerable fathers stood
And gazed through misty centuries
As far as even Memory sees.
When Britain's eldest first beheld
The light, my fathers then were old.
You of the splendid ancestry,
Who boast about your family tree,

Consider, stranger, this of mine—
Bethink the lineage of a Pine.

Douglas Malloch

THE FATE OF THE OAK

The owl to her mate is calling;
    The river his hoarse song sings;
But the oak is marked for falling,
    That has stood for a hundred springs.
Hark! a blow, and a dull sound follows;
    A second—he bows his head;
A third—and the wood's dark hollows
    Now know that their king is dead.

His arms from their trunk are riven;
    His body all barked and squared;
And he's now, like a felon, driven
    In chains to the strong dock-yard!
He's sawn through the middle, and turned
    For the ribs of a frigate free;
And he's caulked, and pitched, and burned;
    And now—he is fit for sea!

Oh! now—with his wings outspread
    Like a ghost (if a ghost may be),
He will triumph again, though dead,
    And be dreaded in every sea:
The lightning will blaze about,
    And wrap him in flaming pride:
And the thunder-loud cannon will shout,
In the fight, from his bold broadside.

154

ARBOR DAY

And when he has fought, and won,
    And been honoured from shore to shore;
And his journey on earth is done,—
    Why, what can he ask for more?
There is nought that a king can claim,
    Or a poet or warrior bold,
Save a rhyme and a short-lived name,
    And to mix with the common mould!

                    Barry Cornwall

THE FIR-TREE

O singing Wind
Searching field and wood,
    Canst thou find
Aught that's sweet or good,—
Flowers, to kiss awake,
Or dewy grass, to shake,
    Or feathered seed
    Aloft to speed?

Replies the wind:
"I cannot find
Flowers, to kiss awake,
Or dewy grass to shake,

Or feathered seed
Aloft to speed;
Yet I meet
Something sweet,
When the scented fir—
Balsam-breathing fir—
In my flight I stir.

Edith M. Thomas

Included by permission of Houghton Mifflin Company.

GREEN THINGS GROWING

O the green things growing, the green things growing,
The faint sweet smell of the green things growing!
I should like to live, whether I smile or grieve,
Just to watch the happy life of my green things
    growing.

O the fluttering and the pattering of those green things
    growing!
How they talk each to each, when none of us are
    knowing;
In the wonderful white of the weird moonlight
Or the dim dreamy dawn when the cocks are crowing.

I love, I love them so—my green things growing!
And I think that they love me, without false showing;

156

ARBOR DAY

For by many a tender touch, they comfort me so much,
With the soft mute comfort of green things growing.

And in the rich store of their blossoms glowing
Ten for one I take they're on me bestowing:
Oh, I should like to see, if God's will it may be,
Many, many a summer of my green things growing!

But if I must be gathered for the angel's sowing,
Sleep out of sight awhile, like the green things growing,
Though dust to dust return, I think I'll scarcely mourn,
If I may change into green things growing.

Dinah Maria Mulock Craik

THE HEART OF THE TREE

What does he plant who plants a tree?
    He plants the friend of sun and sky;
He plants the flag of breezes free;
The shaft of beauty, towering high;
He plants a home to heaven anigh
    For song and mother-croon of bird
    In hushed and happy twilight heard—
The treble of heaven's harmony—
These things he plants who plants a tree.

157

What does he plant who plants a tree?
    He plants cool shade and tender rain,
  And seed and bud of days to be,
And years that fade and flush again;
He plants the glory of the plain;
  He plants the forest's heritage;
  The harvest of a coming age;
The joy that unborn eyes shall see—
These things he plants who plants a tree.

    What does he plant who plants a tree?
        He plants, in sap and leaf and wood,
  In love of home and loyalty
And far-cast thought of civic good—
His blessings on the neighborhood
  When in the hollow of His hand
  Holds all the growth of all our land—
A nation's growth from sea to sea
Stirs in his heart who plants a tree.

Henry Cuyler Bunner

HIAWATHA'S CANOE

"Give me of your bark, O Birch-tree!
Of your yellow bark, O Birch-tree!
Growing by the rushing river,
Tall and stately in the valley!
I a light canoe will build me,
Build a swift Cheemaun for sailing,
That shall float upon the river,
Like a yellow leaf in Autumn,
Like a yellow water-lily!
     "Lay aside your cloak, O Birch-tree!
Lay aside your white-skin wrapper,
For the Summer-time is coming,
And the sun is warm in heaven,
And you need no white-skin wrapper!"
     Thus aloud cried Hiawatha
In the solitary forest,
By the rushing Taquamenaw,
When the birds were singing gayly,
In the Moon of Leaves were singing,
And the sun, from sleep awaking,
Started up and said, "Behold me!
Gheezis, the great Sun, behold me!"
And the tree with all its branches
Rustled in the breeze of morning,

159

Saying with a sigh of patience,
"Take my cloak, O Hiawatha!"
With his knife the tree he girdled;
Just beneath its lowest branches,
Just above the roots, he cut it,
Till the sap came oozing outward;
Down the trunk, from top to bottom,
Sheer he cleft the bark asunder,
With a wooden wedge he raised it,
Stripped it from the trunk unbroken.
　　"Give me of your boughs, O Cedar!
Of your strong and pliant branches,
My canoe to make more steady,
Make more strong and firm beneath me!"
Through the summit of the Cedar
Went a sound, a cry of horror,
Went a murmur of resistance;
But it whispered, bending downward,
"Take my boughs, O Hiawatha!"
Down he hewed the boughs of cedar,
Shaped them straightway to a framework,
Like two bows he formed and shaped them
Like two bended bows together.
　　"Give me of your roots, O Tamarack!
Of your fibrous roots, O Larch-tree!
My canoe to bind together,

So to bind the ends together
That the water may not enter,
That the river may not wet me!"
    And the Larch, with all its fibres,
Shivered in the air of morning,
Touched his forehead with its tassels,
Said, with one long sigh of sorrow,
"Take them all, O Hiawatha!"
From the earth he tore the fibres,
Tore the tough roots of the Larch-tree,
Closely sewed the bark together,
Bound it closely to the framework,
    "Give me of your balm, O Fir-tree!
Of your balsam and your resin,
So to close the seams together
That the water may not enter,
That the river may not wet me!"
    And the Fir-tree, tall and sombre,
Sobbed through all its robes of darkness,
Rattled like a shore with pebbles,
Answered wailing, answered weeping,
"Take my balm, O Hiawatha!"
And he took the tears of balsam,
Took the resin of the Fir-tree,
Smeared therewith each seam and fissure,
Made each crevice safe from water.

"Give me of your quills, O Hedgehog!
All your quills, O Kagh, the Hedgehog!
I will make a necklace of them,
Make a girdle for my beauty,
And two stars to deck her bosom!"
From a hollow tree the Hedgehog
With his sleepy eyes looked at him,
Shot his shining quills, like arrows,
Saying with a drowsy murmur,
Through the tangle of his whiskers,
"Take my quills, O Hiawatha!"
From the ground the quills he gathered,
All the little shining arrows,
Stained them red and blue and yellow,
With the juice of roots and berries;
Into his canoe he wrought them,
Round its waist a shining girdle,
Round its bows a gleaming necklace,
On its breast two stars resplendent.
Thus the Birch Canoe was builded
In the valley, by the river,
In the bosom of the forest;
And the forest's life was in it,
All its mystery and its magic,
All the lightness of the birch-tree,
All the toughness of the cedar,

ARBOR DAY

All the larch's supple sinews;
And it floated on the river
Like a yellow leaf in Autumn,
Like a yellow water-lily.

Selected

Henry Wadsworth Longfellow

Included by permission of Houghton Mifflin Company.

KINDS OF TREES TO PLANT

The sailing Pine; the Cedar, proud and tall;
   The vine-prop Elm; the Poplar, never dry;
The builder Oak, sole king of forests all;
The Aspen, good for staves; the Cypress, funeral;
The Laurel, meed for mighty conquerors
   And poets sage; the Fir, that weepeth still;
The Willow, worn of hopeless paramours;
   The Yew, obedient to the bender's will;
The Birch, for shafts; the Sallow, for the mill;
The warlike Beech; the Ash, for nothing ill;
The fruitful Apple, and the Platane round;
The carver Holm; the Maple seldom inward sound

Selected

Edmund Spenser

MINE HOST OF THE "GOLDEN APPLES"

A goodly host one day was mine,
A Golden Apple his only sign,
That hung from a long branch, ripe and fine.

My host was the bountiful apple-tree;
He gave me shelter and nourished me
With the best of fare, all fresh and free.

And light-winged guests came not a few,
To his leafy inn, and sipped the dew,
And sang their best songs ere they flew.

I slept at night on a downy bed
Of moss, and my Host benignly spread
His own cool shadow over my head.

When I asked what reckoning there might be,
He shook his broad boughs cheerily:—
A blessing be thine, green Apple-tree!

Thomas Westwood

ARBOR DAY

THE OAK

The monarch oak, the patriarch of the trees,
Shoots slowly up, and spreads by slow degrees;
Three centuries he grows, and three he stays
Supreme in state, and in three more decays.

John Dryden

OH, FAIR TO SEE

Oh, fair to see
Bloom-laden cherry tree,
    Arrayed in sunny white:
  An April day's delight,
Oh, fair to see!

Oh, fair to see
Fruit-laden cherry tree,
    With balls of shining red
    Decking a leafy head,
Oh, fair to see!

Christina G. Rossetti

From "Poems" by Christina G. Rossetti.
Included by permission of The Macmillan Company.

THE PINE

The Elm lets fall its leaves before the frost,
The very oak grows shivering with fear,
The trees are barren when the summer's lost:
But one tree keeps its goodness all the year.

Green pine, unchanging as the days go by,
Thou art thyself beneath whatever sky:
My shelter from all winds, my own strong pine,
'Tis Spring, 'tis Summer, still, while thou art mine.

Augusta Webster

THE PLANTING OF THE APPLE-TREE

Come, let us plant the apple-tree.
Cleave the tough greensward with the spade;
Wide let its hollow bed be made;
There gently lay the roots, and there
Sift the dark mould with kindly care,
And press it o'er them tenderly,
As round the sleeping infant's feet
We softly fold the cradle-sheet;
So plant we the apple-tree.

ARBOR DAY

What plant we in this apple-tree?
Buds, which the breath of summer days
Shall lengthen into leafy sprays;
Boughs where the thrush, with crimson breast,
Shall haunt, and sing, and hide her nest;
  We plant, upon the sunny lea,
A shadow for the noontide hour,
A shelter from the summer shower,
    When we plant the apple-tree.

What plant we in this apple-tree?
Sweets for a hundred flowery springs,
To load the May-wind's restless wings,
When, from the orchard-row, it pours
Its fragrance through our open doors:
  A world of blossoms for the bee,
Flowers for the sick girl's silent room,
For the glad infant sprigs of bloom,
    We plant with the apple-tree.

What plant we in this apple-tree?
Fruits that shall swell in sunny June,
And redden in the August noon,
And drop, when gentle airs come by,
That fan the blue September sky,

While children come, with cries of glee,
And seek them where the fragrant grass
Betrays their bed to those who pass,
At the foot of the apple-tree.

.   .   .

William Cullen Bryant

From "The Poetical Works of William Cullen Bryant."
Included by permission of D. Appleton and Company, New York.

PLOUGHMAN AT THE PLOUGH

He behind the straight plough stands
Stalwart, firm shafts in firm hands.

Naught he cares for wars and naught
For the fierce disease of thought.

Only for the winds, the sheer
Naked impulse of the year,

Only for the soil which stares
Clean into God's face he cares.

In the stark might of his deed
There is more than art or creed;

In his wrist more strength is hid
Than in the monstrous Pyramid;

ARBOR DAY

Stauncher than stern Everest
Be the muscles of his breast;

Not the Atlantic sweeps a flood
Potent as the ploughman's blood.

He, his horse, his ploughshare, these
Are the only verities.

Dawn to dusk with God he stands,
The Earth poised on his broad hands.

Louis Golding

Included by permission of the author.

THE POPLARS

My poplars are like ladies trim,
Each conscious of her own estate;
In costume somewhat over prim,
In manner cordially sedate.
Like two old neighbors met to chat
Beside my garden gate.

My stately old aristocrats—
I fancy still their talk must be
Of rose-conserves and Persian cats,

169

And lavender and Indian tea;—
I wonder sometimes as I pass—
If they approve of me.

I give them greeting night and morn,
I like to think they answer, too,
With that benign assurance born
When youth gives age the reverence due.
And bend their wise heads as I go
As courteous ladies do.

Long may you stand before my door,
Oh, kindly neighbors garbed in green,
And bend with rustling welcome o'er
The many friends who pass between;
And where the little children play
Look down with gracious mien.

Theodosia Garrison

Included by permission of the author.

POPLARS

The poplar is a lonely tree,
It has no branches spreading wide
Where birds may sing or squirrels hide.

ARBOR DAY

It throws no shadow on the grass
Tempting the wayfarers who pass
To stop and sit there quietly.

The poplar is a slender tree,
It has no boughs where children try
To climb far off into the sky,
To hold a swing it's far too weak,
Too small it is for hide-and-seek,
Friendless, forsaken it must be.

The poplar is a restless tree,
At every breeze its branches bend
And signal to the child "Come, friend."
Its leaves forever whispering
To thrush and robin, "Stay and sing,"
They pass. It quivers plaintively.

Poplars are lonely. They must grow
Close to each other in a row.

Edward Bliss Reed

*From "Sea Moods and Other Poems" by Edward Bliss Reed.
Included by permission of Yale University Press.*

SHADE

The kindliest thing God ever made,
His hand of very healing laid
Upon a fevered world, is shade.

His glorious company of trees
Throw out their mantles, and on these
The dust-stained wanderer finds ease.

Green temples, closed against the beat
Of noontime's blinding glare and heat,
Open to any pilgrim's feet.

The white road blisters in the sun;
Now, half the weary journey done,
Enter and rest, Oh, weary one!

And feel the dew of dawn still wet
Beneath thy feet, and so forget
The burning highway's ache and fret.

This is God's hospitality,
And whoso rests beneath a tree
Hath cause to thank Him gratefully.

Theodosia Garrison

Included by permission of the author.

SONG

For the tender beech and the sapling oak,
    That grow by the shadowy rill,
You may cut down both at a single stroke,
    You may cut down which you will.

ARBOR DAY

But this you must know, that as long as they grow,
    Whatever change may be,
You can never teach either oak or beech
    To be aught but a greenwood tree.

Thomas Love Peacock

THE SONG OF THE FOREST RANGER

    Oh, to feel the fresh breeze blowing
        From lone ridges yet untrod!
    Oh, to see the far peak growing
        Whiter as it climbs to God!

    Where the silver streamlet rushes
        I would follow—follow on
    Till I heard the happy thrushes
        Piping lyrics to the dawn.

    I would hear the wild rejoicing
        Of the wind-blown cedar tree,
    Hear the sturdy hemlock voicing
        Ancient epics of the sea.

    Forest aisles would I be winding,
        Out beyond the gates of Care;
    And, in dim cathedrals, finding
        Silence at the shrine of Prayer.

173

When the mystic night comes stealing
  Through my vast green room afar,
Never king had richer ceiling—
  Bended bough and yellow star!

Ah, to list the sacred preaching
  Of the forest's faithful fir,
With his strong arms upward reaching—
  Mighty, trustful worshipper!

Come and learn the joy of living!
  Come and you will understand
How the sun his gold is giving
  With a great, impartial hand!

How the patient pine is climbing,
  Year by year to gain the sky;
How the rill makes sweetest rhyming.
  Where the deepest shadows lie.

I am nearer the great Giver,
  Where His handiwork is crude;
Friend am I of peak and river,
  Comrade of old Solitude.

ARBOR DAY

Not for me the city's riot!
    Not for me the towers of Trade!
I would seek the house of Quiet,
    That the Master Workman made!

Herbert Bashford

Included by permission of the author.

THE SPIRIT OF THE BIRCH

I am the dancer of the wood.
I shimmer in the solitude.
Men call me Birch Tree, yet I know
In other days it was not so.
I am a Dryad slim and white
Who danced too long one summer night,
And the Dawn found and prisoned me!
Captive I moaned my liberty.
But let the wood wind flutes begin
Their elfin music, faint and thin,
I sway, I bend, retreat, advance,
And evermore—I dance! I dance!

Arthur Ketchum

Included by permission of the author.

175

TAPESTRY TREES

Oak

>I am the Roof-tree and the Keel:
>I bridge the seas for woe or weal.

Fir

>High o'er the lordly oak I stand,
>And drive him on from land to land.

Ash

>I heft my brother's iron bane;
>I shaft the spear and build the wain.

Yew

>Dark down the windy dale I grow.
>The father of the fateful Bow.

Poplar

>The warshaft and the milking bowl
>I make, and keep the hay-wain whole

Olive

>The King I bless; the lamps I trim;
>In my warm wave do fishes swim.

Apple-Tree

>I bowed my head to Adam's will;
>The cups of toiling men I fill.

Vine

>I draw the blood from out the earth;
>I store the sun for winter mirth.

176

Orange-Tree

>   Amidst the greenness of my night
>   My odorous lamps hang round and bright.

Fig-Tree

>   I who am little among trees
>   In honey-making mate the bees.

Mulberry-Tree

>   Love's lack hath dyed my berries red:
>   For Love's attire my leaves are shed.

Pear-Tree

>   High o'er the mead-flowers' hidden feet
>   I bear aloft my burden sweet.

Bay

>   Look on my leafy boughs, the Crown
>   Of living song and dead renown!

William Morris

Reprinted by permission from "Poems by the Way" by William Morris—Longmans, Green and Company.

"THERE IS STRENGTH IN THE SOIL"

There is strength in the soil:
In the earth there is laughter and youth.
There is solace and hope in the upturned loam.
And lo, I shall plant my soul in it here like a seed!
And forth it shall come to me as a flower of song:

For I know it is good to get back to the earth
That is orderly, placid, all-patient!
It is good to know how quiet
And noncommittal it breathes,
This ample and opulent bosom
That must some day nurse us all!

Arthur Stringer

Included by permission of the author.

THREE TREES

The pine-tree grew in the wood,
    Tapering, straight, and high;
Stately and proud it stood,
    Black-green against the sky.
Crowded so close, it sought the blue,
And ever upward it reached and grew.

The oak-tree stood in the field.
    Beneath it dozed the herds;
It gave to the mower a shield,
    It gave a home to the birds.
Sturdy and broad, it guarded the farms
With its brawny trunk and knotted arms.

ARBOR DAY

The apple-tree grew by the wall,
  Ugly and crooked and black;
But it knew the gardener's call,
  And the children rode on its back.
It scattered its blossoms upon the air,
It covered the ground with fruitage fair.

"Now, hey," said the pine, "for the wood!
  Come live with the forest band.
Our comrades will do you good,
  And tall and straight you will stand."
And he swung his boughs to a witching sound,
And flung his cones like coins around.

"O-ho!" laughed the sturdy oak;
  "The life of the field for me.
I weather the lightning-stroke;
  My branches are broad and free.
Grow straight and slim in the wood if you will,
Give me the sun and the wind-swept hill."

And the apple-tree murmured low,
  "I am neither straight nor strong;
Crooked my back doth grow
  With bearing my burdens long."
And it dropped its fruit as it dropped a tear,
And reddened the ground with fragrant cheer.

And the Lord of the harvest heard,
    And he said: "I have use for all;
For the bough that shelters the bird,
    For the beam that pillars a hall;
And grow they tall, or grow they ill,
They grow but to wait their Master's will."

So a ship of the oak was sent
    Far over the ocean blue,
And the pine was the mast that bent
    As over the waves it flew,
And the ruddy fruit of the apple-tree
Was borne to a starving isle of the sea.

Now the farmer grows like the oak,
    And the townsman is proud and tall;
The city and field are full of folk—
    But the Lord has need of all.

C. H. Crandall

'TIS MERRY IN GREENWOOD

'Tis merry in greenwood, thus runs the old lay,
In the gladsome month of lively May,
When the wild bird's song on stem and spray
    Invites to forest bower:

Then rears the ash his airy crest,
Then shines the birch in silver vest,
And the beech in glistening leaves is drest,
And dark between shows the oak's proud breast,
    Like a chieftain's frowning tower.

Sir Walter Scott

THE TREE

The tree's early leaf-buds were bursting their brown.
"Shall I take them away?" said the frost sweeping
      down.
   "No; leave them alone
   Till the blossoms have grown,"
Prayed the tree, while he trembled from rootlet to
      crown.

The tree bore his blossoms, and all the birds sung.
"Shall I take them away?" said the wind, as he swung.
   "No; leave them alone
   Till the berries have grown,"
Said the tree, while his leaflets quivering hung.

The tree bore his fruit in the midsummer glow.
Said the child, "May I gather thy berries now?"

"Yes; all thou canst see;
Take them; all are for thee,"
Said the tree, while he bent down his laden boughs
    low.

Björnstjerne Björnson

THE TREE

I love thee when thy swelling buds appear
    And one by one their tender leaves unfold,
As if they knew that warmer suns were near,
    Nor longer sought to hide from winter's cold:
And when with darker growth thy leaves are seen,
    To veil from view the early robin's nest,
I love to lie beneath thy waving screen
    With limbs by summer's heat and toil oppressed;
And when the autumn winds have stripped thee bare,
    And round thee lies the smooth, untrodden snow,
When naught is thine that made thee once so fair,
    I love to watch thy shadowy form below,
And through thy leafless arms to look above
On stars that brighter beam, when most we need their
    love.

Jones Very

TREE BIRTHDAYS

Look! Look at me!
To-day's my birthday, Tree!
See, let me stand up, so,
Beside you.   How you grow!
I'm tall, but oh,
I'll never be as tall as you, I know!
Tree, when's your birthday, please? Why don't you
    speak?
I seem so small,
And you're so tall,
Perhaps you have a birthday every week!

Mary Carolyn Davies

Included by permission of the author.

TREE PLANTING

Oh happy trees that we plant today,
    What great good fortunes wait you!
For you will grow in sun and snow
    Till fruit and flowers freight you.

Your winter covering of snow
    Will dazzle with its splendor;

Your summer's garb with richest glow,
   Will feast of beauty render.

In your cool shade will tired feet
   Pause, weary, when 'tis summer;
And rest like this will be most sweet
   To every tired comer.

Anonymous

TREE-PLANTING

Joy for the sturdy trees;
Fanned by each fragrant breeze,
   Lovely they stand.
The song-birds o'er them trill;
They shade each tinkling rill;
They crown each swelling hill,
   Lowly or grand.

Plant them by stream and way,
Plant them where children play,
   And toilers rest;
In every verdant vale,
On every sunny swale;—
Whether to grow or fail,
   God knoweth best.

184

ARBOR DAY

Select the strong, the fair;
Plant them with earnest care,—
 No toil is vain;
Plant in a fitter place,
Where, like a lovely face
Set in some sweeter grace,
 Change may prove gain.

God will his blessing send;
All things on Him depend,—
 His loving care
Clings to each leaf and flower,
Like ivy to its tower,—
His presence and His power
 Are everywhere.

Samuel Francis Smith

TREES

In the Garden of Eden, planted by God,
There were goodly trees in the springing sod,—

Trees of beauty and height and grace,
To stand in splendor before His face.

Apple and hickory, ash and pear,
Oak and beech and the tulip rare,

The trembling aspen, the noble pine,
The sweeping elm by the river line;

Trees for the birds to build and sing,
And the lilac tree for a joy in spring;

Trees to turn at the frosty call
And carpet the ground for their Lord's footfall;

Trees for fruitage and fire and shade,
Trees for the cunning builder's trade;

Wood for the bow, the spear, and the flail,
The keel and the mast of the daring sail;

He made them of every grain and girth,
For the use of man in the Garden of Earth.

Then lest the soul should not lift her eyes
From the gift to the Giver of Paradise,

On the crown of a hill, for all to see,
God planted a scarlet maple tree.

Bliss Carman

Included by permission of the author and Small, Maynard & Company.

THE   TREES

There's something in a noble tree—
    What shall I say? a soul?
For 'tis not form, or aught we see
    In leaf or branch or bole.
Some presence, though not understood,
    Dwells there alway, and seems
To be acquainted with our mood,
    And mingles in our dreams.

I would not say that trees at all
    Were of our blood and race,
Yet, lingering where their shadows fall,
    I sometimes think I trace
A kinship, whose far-reaching root
    Grew when the world began,
And made them best of all things mute
    To be the friends of man.

Held down by whatsoever might
    Unto an earthly sod,
They stretch forth arms for air and light,
    As we do after God;
And when in all their boughs the breeze
    Moans loud, or softly sings,
As our own hearts in us, the trees
    Are almost human things.

What wonder in the days that burned
    With old poetic dream,
Dead Phaethon's fair sisters turned
    To poplars by the stream!
In many a light cotillion stept
    The trees when fluters blew;
And many a tear, 'tis said, they wept
    For human sorrow too.

Mute, said I? They are seldom thus;
    They whisper each to each,
And each and all of them to us,
    In varied forms of speech.
"Be serious," the solemn pine
    Is saying overhead;
"Be beautiful," the elm-tree fine
    Has always finely said;

"Be quick to feel," the aspen still
    Repeats the whole day long;
While, from the green slope of the hill,
    The oak-tree adds, "Be strong."
When with my burden, as I hear
    Their distant voices call,
I rise, and listen, and draw near,
    "Be patient," say, they all.

                    Samuel Valentine Cole

Included by permission of the author.

TREES

The Oak is called the King of Trees,
The Aspen quivers in the breeze,
The Poplar grows up straight and tall,
The Pear-tree spreads along the wall,
The Sycamore gives pleasant shade,
The Willow droops in watery glade,
The Fir-tree useful timber gives,
The Beech amid the forest lives.

Sara Coleridge

TREES

Of all the trees in England,
    Her sweet three corners in,
Only the Ash, the bonnie Ash,
    Burns sweet while it is green.

Of all the trees in England,
    From sea to sea again,
The Willow loveliest stoops her boughs
    Beneath the driving rain.

Of all the trees in England,
    Past frankincense and myrrh,
There's none for smell, of bloom and smoke,
    Like Lime and Juniper.

Of all the trees in England,
    Oak, Elder, Elm and Thorn,
The Yew alone burns lamps of peace
    For them that lie forlorn.

Walter De La Mare

Included by permission of the author and James B. Pinker & Son.

THE TREES

Time is never wasted, listening to the trees;
If to heaven as grandly we arose as these,
Holding toward each other half their kindly grace,
Haply we were worthier of our human place.

Bending down to meet you on the hillside path,
Birch and oak and maple each his welcome hath;
Each his own fine cadence, his familiar word,
By the ear accustomed, always plainly heard.

Every tree gives answer to some different mood:
This one helps you, climbing; that for rest is good:

ARBOR DAY

Beckoning friends, companions, sentinels, they are;
Good to live and die with, good to greet afar.

Take a poet with you when you seek their shade,—
One whose verse like music in a tree is made;
Yet your mind will wander from his rarest lay,
Lost in rhythmic measures that above you sway.

Leafy light and shadow flit across the book;
Flickering, swift suggestions; word, and thought, and
    look
Of a subtle Presence writing nobler things
On his open pages, than the poet sings.

They are poets, also; winds that turn their leaves
Waken a responsive tone that laughs or grieves;
As your thoughts within you changefully are stirred,
Prophecy or promise, lilt or hymn, is heard.

Never yet has poet sung a perfect song,
But his life was rooted like a tree's, among
Earth's great, feeding forces,—even as crag and
    mould,
Rhythms that stir the forest by firm fibres hold.

Harmonies ethereal haunt his topmost bough,
Upward from the mortal drawn, he knows not how:
The old, sacred story of celestial birth
Rising from terrestrial; heaven revealed through earth.

191

Dear, inspiring, friendly dwellers of the wood,
Always reaching downward something grand or good
From the lofty spaces where you breathe and live;
Royally unconscious, careless what you give!

O ye glorious creatures, heirs with us of earth!
Might we win the secret of our loftier birth,—
From our depths of being grow like you, and climb
To our heights of blessing,—life would be sublime'

Lucy Larcom

Included by permission of Houghton Mifflin Company.

THE TREES

The poplar is a French tree,
A tall and laughing wench tree,
A slender tree, a tender tree,
That whispers to the rain—
An easy, breezy flapper tree,
A lithe and blithe and dapper tree,
A girl of trees, a pearl of trees,
Beside the shallow Aisne.

The oak is a British tree,
And not at all a skittish tree;
A rough tree, a tough tree,
A knotty tree to bruise;

192

ARBOR DAY

A drives-his-roots-in-deep tree,
A what-I-find-I-keep tree,
A mighty tree, a blighty tree,
A tree of stubborn thews.

The pine tree is our own tree,
A grown tree, a cone tree,
The tree to face a bitter wind,
The tree for mast and spar—
A mountain tree, a fine tree,
A fragrant turpentine tree,
A limber tree, a timber tree,
And resinous with tar!

Christopher Morley

Included by permission of the author.

UNDER THE GREENWOOD TREE

Under the greenwood tree,
Who loves to lye with me,
And turne his merrie Note
Unto the sweet Bird's throte:
Come hither, come hither, come hither,
Heere shall he see no enemie
But Winter and rough Weather.

Who doth ambition shunne
And loves to live i' the Sunne,
Seeking the food he eates
And pleased with what he gets:
Come hither, come hither, come hither,
  Heere shall he see no enemie
But Winter and rough Weather.

William Shakespeare

WHAT DO WE PLANT WHEN WE PLANT THE TREE

What do we plant when we plant the tree?
We plant the ship which will cross the sea,
We plant the mast to carry the sails,
We plant the planks to withstand the gales—
The keel, the keelson, and beam and knee,—
We plant the ship when we plant the tree.

What do we plant when we plant the tree?
We plant the house for you and me.
We plant the rafters, the shingles, the floors,
We plant the studding, the lath, the doors,
The beams and siding, all parts that be,
We plant the house when we plant the tree.

194

ARBOR DAY

What do we plant when we plant the tree?
A thousand things that we daily see.
We plant the spire that out-towers the crag,
We plant the staff for our country's flag,
We plant the shade from the hot sun free;
We plant all these when we plant the tree.

Henry Abbey

THE WILLOWS

By the little river,
    Still and deep and brown,
Grow the graceful willows,
    Gently dipping down;

Dipping down and brushing
    Everything that floats—
Leaves and logs and fishes,
    And the passing boats.

Were they water maidens
    In the long ago,
That they lean out sadly
    Looking down below?

In the misty twilight
　　You can see their hair,
Weeping water maidens
　　That were once so fair.

Walter Prichard Eaton

Included by permission of the author and George H. Doran Company.

WOODMAN, SPARE THAT TREE

Woodman, spare that tree!
　　Touch not a single bough!
In youth it sheltered me,
　　And I'll protect it now.
'Twas my forefather's hand
　　That placed it near his cot;
There, woodman, let it stand,
　　Thy axe shall harm it not!

That old familiar tree,
　　Whose glory and renown
Are spread o'er land and sea—
　　And wouldst thou hew it down?
Woodman, forbear thy stroke!
　　Cut not its earth-bound ties;
Oh, spare that aged oak,
　　Now towering to the skies!

ARBOR DAY

When but an idle boy
    I sought its grateful shade;
In all their gushing joy
    Here, too, my sisters played.
My mother kissed me here;
    My father pressed my hand—
Forgive this foolish tear,
    But let that old oak stand!

My heart-strings round thee cling,
    Close as thy bark, old friend!
Here shall the wild-bird sing,
    And still thy branches bend,
Old tree! the storm still brave!
    And, woodman, leave the spot;
While I've a chance to save,
    Thy axe shall harm it not.

George P. Morris

WOODNOTES

As the sunbeams stream through liberal space
And nothing jostle or displace,
So waved the pine-tree through my thought
And fanned the dreams it never brought.
"Whether is better, the gift or the donor?
Come to me,"

Quoth the pine-tree,
"I am the giver of honor.
My garden is the cloven rock,
And my manure the snow;
And drifting sand-heaps feed my stock,
In summer's scorching glow.
He is great who can live by me:
The rough and bearded forester
Is better than the lord;
God fills the scrip and canister,
Sin piles the loaded board.
The lord is the peasant that was,
The peasant the lord that shall be;
The lord is hay, the peasant grass,
One dry, and one the living tree.
Who liveth by the ragged pine
Foundeth a heroic line;
Who liveth in the palace hall
Waneth fast and spendeth all.
He goes to my savage haunts,
With his chariot and his care;
My twilight realm he disenchants,
And finds his prison there.
"What prizes the town and the tower?
Only what the pine-tree yields;
Sinew that subdued the fields;
The wild-eyed boy, who in the woods

Chants his hymn to hills and floods,
Whom the city's poisoning spleen
Made not pale, or fat, or lean;
Whom the rain and the wind purgeth,
Whom the dawn and the day-star urgeth,
In whose cheek the rose-leaf blusheth,
In whose feet the lion rusheth.
Iron arms and iron mold,
That know not fear, fatigue or cold.
I give my rafters to his boat,
My billets to his boiler's throat,
And I will swim the ancient sea
To float my child to victory,
And grant to dwellers with the pine
Dominion o'er the palm and vine.
Who leaves the pine-tree leaves his friend,
Unnerves his strength, invites his end.
Cut a bough from my parent stem,
And dip it in thy porcelain vase;
A little while each russet gem
Will swell and rise with wonted grace;
But when it seeks enlarged supplies,
The orphan of the forest dies.
Whoso walks in solitude
And inhabiteth the wood,
Choosing light, wave, rock and bird,
Before the money-loving herd,

Into that forester shall pass,
From these companions, power and grace.
Clean shall he be, without, within,
From the old adhering sin,
All ill dissolving in the light
Of this triumphant piercing sight:
Not vain, nor sour, nor frivolous;
Not mad, athirst nor garrulous;
Grave, chaste, contented, though retired,
And of all other men desired.
On him the light of star and moon
Shall fall with purer radiance down;
All constellations of the sky
Shed their virtue through his eye.
Him nature giveth for defense
His formidable innocence;
The mountain sap, the shells, the sea,
All spheres, all stones, his helpers be;
He shall meet the speeding year,
Without wailing, without fear;
He shall be happy in his love,
Like to like shall joyful prove;
He shall be happy whilst he woos,
Muse-born, a daughter of the Muse "

Ralph Waldo Emerson

(Selected)

Included by permission of Houghton Mifflin Company.

MOTHER'S DAY IN POETRY

Hundreds of dewdrops to greet the dawn,
      Hundreds of bees in the purple clover,
Hundreds of butterflies on the lawn,
      But only one mother the wide world over.

Anonymous

THE BABY

Safe sleeping on its mother's breast
    The smiling babe appears,
Now sweetly sinking into rest;
    Now washed in sudden tears:
Hush, hush, my little baby dear,
There's nobody to hurt you here.

Without a mother's tender care,
    The little thing must die,
Its chubby hands too feeble are
    One service to supply;
And not a tittle does it know
What kind of world 'tis come into.

The lambs sport gayly on the grass
    When scarcely born a day;
The foal, beside its mother ass,
    Trots frolicksome away,
No other creature, tame or wild,
Is half so helpless as a child.

To nurse the Dolly, gayly drest,
    And stroke its flaxen hair,

Or ring the coral at its waist,
　With silver bells so fair,
Is all the little creature can,
That is so soon to be a man.

Full many a summer's sun must glow
　And lighten up the skies,
Before its tender limbs can grow
　To anything of size;
And all the while the mother's eye
Must every little want supply.

Then surely, when each little limb
　Shall grow to healthy size,
And youth and manhood strengthen him
　For toil and enterprise,
His mother's kindness is a debt,
He never, never will forget.

Ann Taylor

*From "Original Poems" by Ann and Jane Taylor.
Included by permission of Frederick A. Stokes Company.*

THE BIRD'S NEST

Eliza and Anne were extremely distress'd
To see an old bird fly away from her nest,
　And leave her poor young ones alone;

MOTHER'S DAY

The pitiful chirping they heard from the tree
Made them think it as cruel as cruel could be,
   Not knowing for what she had flown.

But, when with a worm in her bill she return'd,
They smil'd on each other, soon having discern'd
   She had not forsaken her brood;
But like their dear mother was careful and kind,
Still thinking of them, though she left them behind
   To seek for them suitable food.

Elizabeth Turner

A BOY'S MOTHER

My mother she's so good to me
Ef I was good as I could be,
I couldn't be as good—no, sir!—
Can't any boy be good as her!

She loves me when I'm glad er sad;
She loves me when I'm good er bad;
An', what's a funniest thing, she says
She loves me when she punishes.

I don't like her to punish me—
That don't hurt,—but it hurts to see
Her cryin'.—Nen I cry; an' nen
We both cry an' be good again.

She loves me when she cuts an' sews
My little cloak an' Sunday clothes;
An' when my Pa comes home to tea,
She loves him most as much as me.

She laughs an' tells him all I said,
An' grabs me up an' pats my head;
An' I hug her, an' hug my Pa
An' love him purt'nigh much as Ma.

James Whitcomb Riley

From *Neighborly Poems. Copyright* 1890-1918.
Used by special permission of the publishers, The Bobbs-Merrill Company.

EVENING SONG

Little birds sleep sweetly
    In their soft round nests,
Crouching in the cover
    Of their mothers' breasts.

MOTHER'S DAY

Little lambs lie quiet,
    All the summer night,
With their old ewe mothers,
    Warm, and soft, and white.

But more sweet and quiet
    Lie our little heads,
With our own dear mothers
    Sitting by our beds;
And their soft sweet voices
    Sing our hush-a-bies,
While the room grows darker,
    As we shut our eyes.

And we play at evening
    Round our fathers' knees;
Birds are not so merry,
    Singing on the trees;
Lambs are not so happy,
    'Mid the meadow flowers;
They have play and pleasure,
    But not love like ours.

Cecil Frances Alexander

THE FAIRY-BOOK

In summer, when the grass is thick, if Mother has the
    time,
She shows me with her pencil how a poet makes a
    rhyme
And often she is sweet enough to choose a leafy nook,
Where I cuddle up so closely while she reads the
    Fairy-book.

In winter, when the corn's asleep, and birds are not in
    song,
And crocuses and violets have been away too long,
Dear Mother puts her thimble by in answer to my look,
And I cuddle up so closely while she reads the Fairy-
    book.

And Mother tells the servants that they really must
    contrive
To manage all the household things, because at half-
    past five
We cannot spare a second for the housemaid or the
    cook
While we cuddle close together with the happy Fairy-
    book.

Norman Gale

By permission of the author, Mr. Norman Gale.

HER MOTHER

Oh, if I could only make you see
    The clear blue eyes, the tender smile,
The sovereign sweetness, the gentle grace,
The woman's soul, and the angel's face
    That are beaming on me all the while,
I need not speak these foolish words:
Yet one word tells you all I would say,—
She is my mother: you will agree
That all the rest may be thrown away.

Alice Cary

HIS MOTHER IN HER HOOD OF BLUE

When Jesus was a little thing,
    His mother, in her hood of blue,
Called to Him through the dusk of spring:
    "Jesus, my Jesus, where are you?"

Caught in a gust of whirling bloom,
    She stood a moment at the door,
Then lit the candle in the room,
    In its pink earthen bowl of yore.

The little Jesus saw it all:—
    The blur of yellow in the street;
The fair trees by the tumbling wall:
    The shadowy other lads, whose feet

Struck a quick noise from out the grass:
    He saw, dim in the half-lit air,
As one sees folk within a glass,
    His mother with her candle there.
Jesus! Jesus!

When he a weary man became,
    I think, as He went to and fro,
He heard her calling just the same
    Across that dusk of long ago.
Jesus!

For men were tired that had been bold:—
    And strange indeed this should befall—
One day so hot, one day so cold—
    But mothers never change at all.
Jesus!

Lizette Woodworth Reese

Included by permission of the author and Thomas B. Mosher, publisher.

"HOW'S MY BOY?"

"Ho, sailor of the sea!
How's my boy—my boy?"
"What's your boy's name, good wife,
And in what good ship sailed he?"
"My boy John—
He that went to sea—
What care I for the ship, sailor?
My boy's my boy to me.

"You come back from sea
And not know my John!
I might as well have asked some landsman
Yonder down in the town.
There's not an ass in all the parish
But he knows my John.

"How's my boy—my boy?
And unless you let me know,
I'll swear you are no sailor,
Blue jacket or no,
Brass button or no, sailor,
Anchor and crown or no!
Sure his ship was the Jolly Briton."—
"Speak low, woman, speak low!"

"And why should I speak low, sailor,
About my own boy John?
If I was loud as I am proud
I'd sing him o'er the town!
Why should I speak low, sailor?"
"That good ship went down."

"How's my boy—my boy?
What care I for the ship, sailor,
I never was aboard her.
Be she afloat, or be she aground,
Sinking or swimming, I'll be bound,
Her owners can afford her!
I say, how's my John?"
"Every man on board went down,
Every man aboard her."

"How's my boy—my boy?
What care I for the men, sailor?
I'm not their mother—
How's my boy—my boy?
Tell me of him and no other!
How's my boy—my boy?"

Sydney Dobell

IF I HAD BUT TWO LITTLE WINGS

If I had but two little wings
 And were a little feathery bird,
  To you I'd fly, my dear!
But thoughts like these are idle things,
  And I stay here.

But in my sleep to you I fly:
 I'm always with you in my sleep!
  The world is all one's own.
But then one wakes, and where am I?
  All, all alone.

Sleep stays not, though a monarch bids:
 So I love to wake ere break of day:
  For though my sleep be gone,
Yet while 'tis dark, one shuts one's lids,
  And still dreams on.

     Samuel Taylor Coleridge

THE JUSTIFIED MOTHER OF MEN

Behold a woman!
 She looks out from her Quaker-cap—her face is
  clearer and more beautiful than the sky.
She sits in an arm-chair, under the shaded porch of
  the farmhouse,
The sun just shines on her old white head.

Her ample gown is of cream-hued linen:
Her grandsons raised the flax and her granddaughters
      spun it with the distaff and wheel.

The melodious character of the earth,
The finish beyond which philosophy cannot go, and
      does not wish to go.
The justified mother of men.

Walt Whitman

LINES ON RECEIVING HIS MOTHER'S PICTURE

O that those lips had language! Life has passed
With me but roughly since I heard thee last.
The same that oft in childhood solaced me;
Voice only fails, else how distinct they say,
"Grieve not, my child—chase all thy fears away!"

.   .   .   .

Children not thine have trod my nursery floor;
And where the gardener Robin, day by day,
Drew me to school along the public way,
Delighted with my bauble coach, and wrapped

MOTHER'S DAY

In scarlet mantle warm, and velvet capped,
'Tis now become a history little known,
That once we called the pastoral house our own.
Short-lived possession! but the record fair
That memory keeps, of all thy kindness there,
Still outlives many a storm, that has effaced
A thousand other themes less deeply traced.
Thy nightly visits to my chamber made,
That thou mightst know me safe and warmly laid;
Thy morning bounties ere I left my home,
The biscuit, or confectionary plum;
The fragrant waters on my cheek bestowed
By thine own hand, till fresh they shone and glowed;
All this, and more endearing still than all,
Thy constant flow of love, that knew no fall. . .

William Cowper

THE LITTLE FISH THAT WOULD
NOT DO AS IT WAS BID

"Dear Mother," said a little fish,
    "Pray is not that a fly?
I'm very hungry, and I wish
    You'd let me go and try."

"Sweet innocent," the mother cried,
    And started from her nook,
"That horrid fly is put to hide
    The sharpness of the hook."

Now, as I've heard, this little trout
    Was young and foolish, too,
And so he thought he'd venture out,
    To see if it were true.

And round about the hook he played,
    With many a longing look,
And—"Dear me," to himself he said,
    "I'm sure that's not a hook.

"I can but give one little pluck:
    Let's see, and so I will."
So on he went, and lo! it stuck
    Quite through his little gill.

And as he faint and fainter grew,
    With hollow voice he cried,
"Dear mother, had I minded you,
    I need not now have died."

Jane and Ann Taylor

From "Original Poems" by Jane and Ann Taylor.
Included by permission of G. P. Putnam's Sons.

MATER AMABILIS

Down the goldenest of streams,
    Tide of dreams,
The fair cradled man-child drifts;
Sways with cadenced motion slow,
    To and fro,
As the mother-foot, poised lightly, falls and lifts.

He, the firstling,—he, the light
    Of her sight,—
He, the breathing pledge of love,
'Neath the holy passion lies,
    Of her eyes,—
Smiles to feel the warm, life-giving ray above

She believes that in his vision,
    Skies elysian
O'er an angel people shine.
Back to gardens of delight,
    Taking flight,
His auroral spirit basks in dreams divine.

But she smiles through anxious tears,
    Unborn years
Pressing forward, she perceives

Shadowy muffled shapes, they come
    Deaf and dumb,
Bringing what? dry chaff and tares,
    Or full-eared sheaves?

What for him shall she invoke?
    Shall the oak
Bind the man's triumphant brow?
Shall his daring foot alight
    On the height?
Shall he dwell amidst the humble and the low?

Through what tears and sweat and pain,
    Must he gain
Fruitage from the tree of life?
Shall it yield him bitter flavor?
    Shall its savor
Be as manna midst the turmoil and the strife?

In his cradle slept and smiled
    Thus the child
Who as Prince of Peace was hailed.
Thus anigh the mother breast,
    Lulled to rest,
Child-Napoleon down the lillied river sailed.

Crowned or crucified—the same
    Glows the flame
Of her deathless love divine.

MOTHER'S DAY

Still the blessed mother stands,
    In all lands
As she watched beside thy cradle and by mine.

Whatso gifts the years bestow,
    Still men know,
While breathes, lives one who sees
(Stand they pure or sin-defiled)
    But the child
Whom she crooned to sleep and rocked upon
    her knees.

Emma Lazarus

MATERNITY

Heigh ho! daisies and buttercups,
    Fair yellow daffodils, stately and tall,
When the wind wakes how they rock in the grasses,
    And dance with the cockoo-buds, slender and
        small:
Here's two bonny boys, and here's mother's own lasses,
    Eager to gather them all.

Heigh ho! daisies and buttercups,
    Mother shall thread them a daisy chain;
Sing them a song of the pretty hedge-sparrow,
    That loved her brown little ones, loved them full
        fain;

Sing, "Heart thou art wide though the house be but
        narrow"—
    Sing once, and sing it again.

Heigh ho! daisies and buttercups,
    Sweet wagging cowslips, they bend and they bow;
A ship sails afar over warm ocean waters,
    And haply one musing doth stand at her prow.
O bonny brown sons, and O sweet little daughters,
    Maybe he thinks on you now!

Heigh ho! daisies and buttercups,
    Fair yellow daffodils stately and tall;
A sunshiny world full of laughter and leisure,
    And fresh hearts unconscious of sorrow and thrall,
Send down on their pleasure smiles passing its
    measure—
    God that is over us all.

Jean Ingelow

THE MOTHER

From out the South the genial breezes sigh,
They shake the bramble branches to and fro
Whose lovely green delights the gazer's eye:
A mother's thoughts are troubled even so.

220

MOTHER'S DAY

From out the South the genial breezes move,
They shake the branches of the bramble tree:
Unless the sons fair men and honest prove,
The virtuous mother will dishonored be.

The frigid fount with violence the spray
By Shiyoun's town upcasts its watery store:
Though full seven sons she gave to life and day,
The mother's heart is but disturbed the more.

When sings the redbreast, it is bliss to hear,
The dulcet notes the little songster breeds;
But ah! more blissful to a mother's ear,
The fair report of seven good children's deeds.
Translated from the Chinese by George Barrow

MOTHER

I have praised many loved ones in my song,
    And yet I stand
Before her shrine, to whom all things belong,
    With empty hand.

Perhaps the ripening future holds a time
    For things unsaid;
Not now; men do not celebrate in rhyme
    Their daily bread.
Theresa Helburn

Included by permission of the author.

MOTHER
(*From "Snow Bound"*)

Our mother, while she turned her wheel
   Or ran the new-knit stocking-heel,
Told how the Indian hordes came down
At midnight on Cocheco town,
And how her own great-uncle bore
His cruel scalp-mark to fourscore.
Recalling, in her fitting phrase,
   So rich and picturesque and free,
   (The common unrhymed poetry
Of simple life and country ways,)
The story of her early days,—
She made us welcome to her home;
Old hearths grew wide to give us room;
We stole with her a frightened look
At the gray wizard's conjuring-book,
The fame whereof went far and wide
Through all the simple country side;
We heard the hawks at twilight play,
The boat-horn on Piscataqua,
The loon's weird laughter far away;
We fished her little trout-brook, knew
What flowers in wood and meadow grew,
What sunny hillsides autumn-brown

MOTHER'S DAY

She climbed to shake the ripe nuts down,
Saw where in sheltered cove and bay
The ducks' black squadron anchored lay,
And heard the wild-geese calling loud
Beneath the gray November cloud.

John Greenleaf Whittier

THE MOTHER IN THE HOUSE

For such as you, I do believe,
Spirits their softest carpets weave,
And spread them out with gracious hand
Wherever you walk, wherever you stand.

For such as you, of scent and dew
Spirits their rarest nectar brew,
And where you sit and where you sup
Pour beauty's elixir in your cup.

For all day long, like other folk,
You bear the burden, wear the yoke,
And yet when I look in your eyes at eve
You are lovelier than ever, I do believe.

Hermann Hagedorn

Included by special permission of the author.

A MOTHER'S BIRTHDAY

Lord Jesus, Thou hast known
    A mother's love and tender care:
And Thou wilt hear,
    While for my own
Mother most dear
I make this birthday prayer.

Protect her life, I pray,
    Who gave the gift of life to me;
And may she know,
    From day to day,
The deepening glow
Of joy that comes from Thee.

As once upon her breast
    Fearless and well content I lay,
So let her heart
    On Thee at rest,
Fell fear depart
And trouble fade away.

Ah, hold her by the hand,
    As once her hand held mine;

MOTHER'S DAY

And though she may
    Not understand
Life's winding way,
Lead her in peace divine.

I cannot pay my debt
    For all the love that she has given;
But Thou, love's Lord,
    Wilt not forget
Her due reward,—
Bless her in earth and heaven.

Henry Van Dyke

From "Poems of Henry Van Dyke."
Copyright, 1911, by Charles Scribner's Sons.
Included by permission of the author.

THE MOTHER'S HYMN

Lord who ordainst for mankind
    Benignant toils and tender cares,
We thank thee for the ties that bind
    The mother to the child she bears.

We thank thee for the hopes that rise
    Within her heart, as, day by day,
The dawning soul, from those young eyes,
    Looks with a clearer, steadier ray.

225

And grateful for the blessing given
    With that dear infant on her knee,
She trains the eye to look to heaven,
    The voice to lisp a prayer to Thee.

Such thanks the blessed Mary gave
    When from her lap the Holy Child,
Sent from on high to seek and save
    The lost of earth, looked up and smiled.

All-Gracious! grant to those who bear
    A mother's charge, the strength and light
To guide the feet that own their care
    In ways of Love and Truth and Right.

William Cullen Bryant

*From "The Poetical Works of William Cullen Bryant."
Included by permission of D. Appleton and Company, New York.*

A MOTHER'S PICTURE

She seemed an angel to our infant eyes!
Once, when the glorifying moon revealed
Her who at evening by our pillow kneeled—
Soft-voiced and golden-haired, from holy skies
Flown to her loves on wings of Paradise—
We looked to see the pinions half-concealed.

MOTHER'S DAY

The Tuscan vines and olives will not yield
Her back to me, who loved her in this wise,
And since have little known her, but have grown
To see another mother, tenderly,
Watch over sleeping darlings of her own;
Perchance the years have changed her: yet alone
This picture lingers: still she seems to me
The fair, young Angel of my infancy.

Edmund Clarence Stedman

Included by permission of Houghton Mifflin Company.

MY MOTHER

I walk upon the rocky shore,
Her strength is in the ocean's roar.
I glance into the shaded pool,
Her mind is there so calm and cool.
I hear sweet rippling of the sea,
Naught but her laughter 'tis to me.
I gaze into the starry skies,
And there I see her wondrous eyes.
I look into my inmost mind,
And here her inspiration find.
In all I am and hear and see,
My precious mother is with me.

Josephine Rice Creelman

MY MOTHER

God made my mother on an April day,
From sorrow and the mist along the sea,
Lost birds' and wanderers' songs and ocean spray,
And the moon loved her wandering jealously.

Beside the ocean's din she combed her hair,
Singing the nocturne of the passing ships,
Before her earthly lover found her there
And kissed away the music from her lips.

She came unto the hills and saw the change
That brings the swallow and the geese in turns.
But there was not a grief she deemed strange,
For there is that in her which always mourns.

Kind heart she has for all on hill or wave
Whose hopes grew wings like ants to fly away.
I bless the God who such a mother gave
This poor bird-hearted singer of a day.

Francis Ledwidge

From "*The Collected Poems of Francis Ledwidge.*"
Included by permission of Brentano's.

228

MY MOTHER

Who fed me from her gentle breast,
And hush'd me in her arms to rest,
And on my cheeks sweet kisses prest?
    My Mother.

When sleep forsook my open eye,
Who was it sang sweet hushaby
And rock'd me that I should not cry?
    My Mother.

Who sat and watched my infant head,
When sleeping on my cradle bed,
And tears of sweet affection shed?
    My Mother.

When pain and sickness made me cry,
Who gaz'd upon my heavy eye,
And wept, for fear that I should die?
    My Mother.

Who drest my doll in clothes so gay,
And taught me pretty how to play,
And minded all I had to say?
    My Mother.

Who ran to help me when I fell,
And would some pretty story tell,
Or kiss the place to make it well?
  My Mother.

Who taught my infant lips to pray,
And love God's holy book and day,
And walk in wisdom's pleasant way?
  My Mother.

And can I ever cease to be
Affectionate and kind to thee,
Who wast so very kind to me,
  My Mother?

Ah! no, the thought I cannot bear,
And if God please my life to spare,
I hope I shall reward thy care,
  My Mother.

When thou art feeble, old, and grey,
My healthy arm shall be thy stay,
And I will soothe thy pains away,
  My Mother.

And when I see thee hang thy head,
'Twill be my turn to watch thy bed,
And tears of sweet affection shed,
  My Mother.

MOTHER'S DAY

For God Who lives above the skies,
Would look with vengeance in His eyes,
If I should ever dare despise
  My Mother.

Ann Taylor

MY SONG

This song of mine will wind its music around you, my child, like the fond arms of love.

This song of mine will touch your forehead like a kiss of blessing.

When you are alone it will sit by your side and whisper in your ear, when you are in the crowd it will fence you about with aloofness.

My song will be like a pair of wings to your dreams, it will transport your heart to the verge of the unknown.

It will be like a faithful star overhead when dark night is over your road.

My song will sit in the pupils of your eyes, and will carry your sight into the heart of things.

And when my voice is silent in death, my song will speak in your living heart.

Rabindranath Tagore

MY TRUST

A picture memory brings to me:
I look across the years and see
Myself beside my mother's knee.

I feel her gentle hand restrain
My selfish moods, and know again
A child's blind sense of wrong and pain.

But wiser now, a man gray grown,
My childhood's needs are better known,
My mother's chastening love I own.

John Greenleaf Whittier

OUR MOTHER

Hundreds of stars in the pretty sky,
　　Hundreds of shells on the shore together,
Hundreds of birds that go singing by,
　　Hundreds of birds in the sunny weather,

Hundreds of dewdrops to greet the dawn,
　　Hundreds of bees in the purple clover,
Hundreds of butterflies on the lawn,
　　But only one mother the wide world over.

Anonymous

232

PARENTHOOD

The birches that dance on the top of the hill
Are so slender and young that they cannot keep still,
They bend and they nod at each whiff of a breeze,
For you see they are still just the children of trees.

But the birches below in the valley are older,
They are calmer and straighter and taller and colder.
Perhaps when we've grown up as solemn and grave,
We, too, will have children who do not behave!

John Farrar

From "Songs for Parents" by John Farrar.
Included by permission of Yale University Press.

A PRAYER FOR A SLEEPING CHILD

Once a wife in Bethlehem
    Had a child like me:
Once she watched a sleepy head
    Held upon her knee,
And, with young eyes dim,
    Now she prayed for him!

Every life holds pain and strife,
    Each life holds delight:
Through their paths' entanglement
    May he walk aright,
Like her, so today
    For my child I pray.

May her Babe, as quick years flow,
    Hand in hand with my child go,
Holding him with loving arm
    Safe from hurt and free from harm.

Mary Carolyn Davies

Included by permission of the author and Woman's Home Companion.

A SONG FOR MY MOTHER—HER HANDS

My mother's hands are cool and fair,
    They can do anything.
Delicate mercies hide them there
    Like flowers in the spring.

When I was small and could not sleep,
    She used to come to me,
And with my cheek upon her hand
    How sure my rest would be.

MOTHER'S DAY

For everything she ever touched
    Of beautiful or fine,
Their memories living in her hands
    Would warm that sleep of mine.

Her hands remember how they played
    One time in meadow streams,—
And all the flickering song and shade
    Of water took my dreams.

Swift through her haunted fingers pass
    Memories of garden things;—
I dipped my face in flowers and grass
    And sounds of hidden wings.

One time she touched the cloud that kissed
    Brown pastures bleak and far:—
I leaned my cheek into a mist
    And thought I was a star.

All this was very long ago
    And I am grown; but yet
The hand that lured my slumber so
    I never can forget.

For still when drowsiness comes on
  It seems so soft and cool,
Shaped happily beneath my cheek,
  Hollow and beautiful.

Anna Hampstead Branch

Included by permission of the author and Houghton Mifflin Company.

A SONG FOR MY MOTHER—HER STORIES

I always liked to go to bed—
  It looked so dear and white.
Besides, my mother used to tell
  A story every night.

When other children cried to go
  I did not mind at all,
She made such faery pageants grow
  Upon the bedroom wall.

The room was full of slumber lights,
  Of seas and ships and wings,
Of Holy Grails and swords and knights
  And beautiful, kind kings.

MOTHER'S DAY

And so she wove and wove and wove
    Her singing thoughts through mine.
I heard them murmuring through my sleep,
    Sweet, audible, and fine.

Beneath my pillow all night long
    I heard her stories sing,
So spun through the enchanted sheet
    Was their soft shadowing.

Dear custom, stronger than the years—
    Then let me not grow dull!
Still every night my bed appears
    Friendly and beautiful!

Even now, when I lie down to sleep,
    It comes like a caress,
And still somehow my childish heart
    Expects a pleasantness.

I find in the remembering sheets
    Old stories, told by her,
And they are sweet as rosemary
    And dim as lavender.

Anna Hampstead Branch

Included by permission of the author and Houghton Mifflin Company.

A SONG FOR MY MOTHER—HER WORDS

My mother has the prettiest tricks
    Of words and words and words.
Her talk comes out as smooth and sleek
    As breasts of singing birds.

She shapes her speech all silver fine
    Because she loves it so.
And her own eyes begin to shine
    To hear her stories grow.

And if she goes to make a call
    Or out to take a walk,
We leave our work when she returns
    And run to hear her talk.

We had not dreamed these things were so
    Of sorrow and of mirth.
Her speech is as a thousand eyes
    Through which we see the earth.

God wove a web of loveliness,
    Of clouds and stars and birds,
But made not anything at all
    So beautiful as words.

MOTHER'S DAY

They shine around our simple earth
    With golden shadowings,
And every common thing they touch
    Is exquisite with wings.

There's nothing poor and nothing small
    But is made fair with them.
They are the hands of living faith
    That touch the garment's hem.

They are as fair as bloom or air,
    They shine like any star,
And I am rich who learned from her
    How beautiful they are.

Anna Hampstead Branch

Included by permission of the author and Houghton Mifflin Company.

TO MY FIRST LOVE, MY MOTHER

Sonnets are full of love, and this my tome
    Has many sonnets: so here now shall be
    One sonnet more, a loving sonnet, from me
To her whose heart is my heart's quiet home,
    To my first Love, my Mother, on whose knee
I learnt love-lore that is not troublesome:
    Whose service is my special dignity
And she my lodestar while I go and come.

And so because you love, and because
  I love you, Mother, I have woven a wreath
    Of rhymes wherewith to crown your honored
      name:
    In you not fourscore years can dim the flame
Of love, whose blessed glow transcends the laws
    Of time and change and mortal life and
      death.

Christina G. Rossetti

From "Poems" by Christina G. Rossetti.
Included by permission of The Macmillan Company.

TO MY MOTHER

They tell us of an Indian tree
  Which howsoe'er the sun and sky
May tempt its boughs to wander free,
  And shoot and blossom, wide and high,
  Downward again to that dear earth
From which the life, that fills and warms
  Its grateful being, first had birth.
'Tis thus, though wooed by flattering friends,
  And fed with fame (if fame it may be),
This heart, my own dear mother, bends,
  With love's true instinct, back to thee!

Thomas Moore

A VALENTINE TO MY MOTHER

My blessed Mother dozing in her chair
    On Christmas Day seemed an embodied Love,
A comfortable Love with soft brown hair
    Softened and silvered to a tint of dove;
A better sort of Venus with an air
    Angelical from thoughts that dwell above;
A wiser Pallas in whose body fair
    Enshrined a blessed soul looks out thereof.
Winter brought holly then; now Spring has brought
    Paler and frailer snowdrops shivering;
And I have brought a simple humble thought—
    I her devoted duteous Valentine— .
A lifelong thought which drills this song I sing,
    A lifelong love to this dear saint of mine.

Christina G. Rossetti

From "Poems" by Christina G. Rossetti.
Included by permission of The Macmillan Company.

THE VOICE

As I went down the hill I heard
    The laughter of the countryside;
For, rain being past, the whole land stirred
    With new emotion, like a bride.

I scarce had left the grassy lane,
    When something made me catch my breath
A woman called, and called again,
    Elizabeth! Elizabeth!

It was my mother's name. A part
    Of wounded memory sprang to tears,
And the few violets of my heart
    Shook in the wind of happier years.
Quicker than magic came the face
    That once was sun and moon for me;
The garden shawl, the cap of lace,
    The collie's head against her knee.

Mother, who findest out a way
    To pass the sentinels, and stand
Behind my chair at close of day,
    To touch me—almost—with thy hand,
Deep in my breast, how sure, how clear,
    The lamp of love burns on till death!—
How trembles if I chance to hear
    Elizabeth! Elizabeth!

Norman Gale

Included by special permission of Mr. Norman Gale.

THE WATCHER

She always leaned to watch for us,
    Anxious if we were late,
In winter by the window,
    In summer by the gate;

And though we mocked her tenderly,
    Who had such foolish care,
The long way home would seem more safe
    Because she waited there.

Her thoughts were all so full of us,
    She never could forget!
And so I think that where she is
    She must be watching yet,

Waiting till we come home to her,
    Anxious if we are late—
Watching from Heaven's window,
    Leaning from Heaven's gate.

Margaret Widdemer

From "Cross Currents" by Margaret Widdemer.
Included by permission of Harcourt, Brace and Company, Inc.

WHAT RULES THE WORLD

They say that man is mighty,
    He governs land and sea,
He wields a mighty scepter
    O'er lesser powers than he;

But mightier power and stronger
    Man from his throne has hurled,
For the hand that rocks the cradle
    Is the hand that rules the world.

W. R. Wallace

WHEN SHE A MAIDEN SLIM

When she, a maiden slim,
Suffered his yoke and bondage, on she took
Smooth matron's ways and dalliance forsook
With gossip-girls in girls' shy eagerness
To wonder at men's deeds; and with the dress
Of wife attuned her heart in graver mood
To bear the sober fruits of Motherhood.
A-many children him in time she bore,
So many treasure-houses for her store

244

Of love, which ever waxed as each new voice
Wailing for succor made her heart rejoice
That she was almoner.

Maurice Hewlett

WHICH LOVED HER BEST?

"I love you, Mother," said little John;
Then, forgetting his work, his cap went on,
And he was off to the garden-swing,
And left her the water and wood to bring.

"I love you, Mother," said rosy Nell—
"I love you better than tongue can tell;"
Then she teased and pouted full half the day
Till her mother rejoiced when she went to play.

"I love you, Mother," said little Fan;
"To-day I'll help you all I can;
How glad I am school doesn't keep!"
So she rocked the babe till it fell asleep.

Then, stepping softly, she fetched the broom
And swept the floor and tidied the room;
Busy and happy all day was she,
Helpful and happy as child could be.

"I love you, Mother," again they said,
Three little children going to bed.
How do you think that mother guessed
Which of them really loved her best?

Anonymous

WISHING

Ring-Ting! I wish I were a Primrose,
A bright yellow Primrose blowing in the spring!
    The stooping boughs above me,
    The wandering bee to love me,
    The fern and moss to creep across,
    And the Elm-tree for our king!

Nay—stay! I wish I were an Elm-tree,
A great lofty Elm-tree, with green leaves gay!
    The winds would set them dancing,
    The sun and moonshine glance in,
    The birds would house among the boughs,
    And sweetly sing!

Oh—no! I wish I were a Robin.
A Robin or a little Wren, everywhere to go;
    Through forest, field or garden,
    And ask no leave or pardon,
    Till winter comes with icy thumbs
    To ruffle up our wing!

246

MOTHER'S DAY

Well—tell! Where should I fly to,
Where go to sleep in the dark wood or dell?
   Before a day was over,
   Home comes the rover,
   For mother's kiss,—sweeter this
   Than any other thing!

William Allingham

MEMORIAL DAY IN POETRY

Lord, let war's tempests cease,
Fold the whole world in peace
    Under Thy wings.
Make all the nations one,
All hearts beneath the sun,
Till Thou shalt reign alone,
    Great King of Kings.

Henry W. Longfellow

THE ANXIOUS DEAD

O guns, fall silent till the dead men hear
    Above their heads the legions pressing on:
(These fought their fight in time of bitter fear
    And died not knowing how the day had gone.)

O flashing muzzles, pause, and let them see
    The coming dawn that streaks the day afar:
Then let your mighty chorus witness be
    To them, and Caesar, that we still make war.

Tell them, O guns, that we have heard their call,
    That we have sworn, and will not turn aside,
That we will onward, till we win or fall,
    That we will keep the faith for which they died.

Bid them be patient, and some day, anon,
    They shall feel earth enwrapt in silence deep,
Shall greet, in wonderment, the quiet dawn,
    And in content may turn them to their sleep.

John McCrae

*From "In Flanders Fields," by John McCrae.
Included by permission of G. P. Putnam's Sons.*

THE ARMORER'S SONG

Let hammer on anvil ring,
And the forge fire brightly shine;
Let wars rage still,
While I work with a will
At this peaceful trade of mine.
The sword is a weapon to conquer fields;
I honor the man who shakes it:
But naught is the lad who the broad-sword wields
Compared to the lad who makes it.

Clang! Clang! Clang!
Then huzzah for the anvil, the forge, and the sledge!
Huzzah for the sparks that fly!
If I had a cup I would straightway pledge
The armorer—that is I!

Let others of glory sing,
As they struggle in glory's quest.
Let them wave their brands
In their mailéd hands,
While the sword smites shield and crest.
Oh, war is a trade I have not essayed,
Though goodliest fame attends it.
I sing of the one who, when fight is done,
Takes every good sword and mends it.

MEMORIAL DAY

Clang! Clang! Clang!
Then huzzah for the valiant, the squire, or the knight
　Who loveth the battle-cry!
But here's to the swordsman that maketh them fight,
　The armorer—that is I!

Harry Bache Smith

Included by permission of the author.

A BALLAD OF HEROES

Because you passed, and now are not,—
　Because, in some remoter day,
Your sacred dust from doubtful spot
　Was blown of ancient airs away,—
　Because you perished,—must men say
Your deeds were naught, and so profane
　Your lives with that cold burden?　Nay,
The deeds you wrought are not in vain!

Though, it may be, above the plot
　That hid your once imperial clay,
No greener than o'er men forgot
　The unregarding grasses sway;—
　Though there no sweeter is the lay
From careless bird,—though you remain
　Without distinction of decay,—
The deeds you wrought are not in vain!

253

No. For while yet in tower or cot
    Your story stirs the pulses' play;
And men forget the sordid lot—
    The sordid care, of cities gray;—
    While yet, beset in homelier fray.
They learn from you the lesson plain
    That Life may go, so Honour stay,—
The deeds you wrought are not in vain!

Envoy

Heroes of old! I humbly lay
    The laurel on your graves again;
Whatever men have done, men may,—
    The deeds you wrought are not in vain.

Austin Dobson

BATTLE HYMN OF THE REPUBLIC

Mine eyes have seen the glory of the coming of the
    Lord;
He is trampling out the vintage where the grapes
    of wrath are stored,
He hath loosed the fateful lightning of His terrible
    swift sword;
        His truth is marching on.

I have seen Him in the watch-fires of a hundred circling
    camps;
They have builded Him an altar in the evening
    dews and damps,
I can read his righteous sentence by the dim and flaring
    lamps;
       His day is marching on.

I have read a fiery gospel, writ in burnished rows of
    steel;
"As ye deal with My contemners, so with you My
    grace shall deal:
Let the Hero, born of woman, crush the serpent with
    his heel,
       Since God is marching on."

He has sounded forth the trumpet that shall never call
    retreat;
He is sifting out the hearts of men before His judgment
    seat:
Oh, be swift, my soul, to answer Him,—be jubilant,
    my feet!
       Our God is marching on.

In the beauty of the lilies Christ was born across the
    sea,
With a glory in His bosom that transfigures you and
    me:

255

As He died to make men holy, let us die to make
    men free,
        While God is marching on.

                        Julia Ward Howe

*Included by permission of, and by special arrangement with, Houghton
Mifflin Company, the authorized publishers.*

THE BATTLEFIELD

They dropped like flakes, they dropped like stars,
    Like petals from a rose,
When suddenly across the June
    A wind with finger goes.

They perished in the seamless grass,—
    No eye could find the place;
But God on his repealless list
    Can summon every face.

                      Emily Dickinson

Included by permission of Martha Dickinson Bianchi.

CORONACH [1]

He is gone on the mountain,
    He is lost to the forest,
Like a summer-dried fountain,
    When our need was the sorest.

MEMORIAL DAY

The font, reappearing,
   From the rain-drops shall borrow,
But to us comes no cheering,
   To Duncan no morrow!

The hand of the reaper
   Takes the ears that are hoary,
But the voice of the weeper
   Wails manhood in glory.
The autumn winds rushing
   Waft the leaves that are serest,
But our flower was in flushing,
   When blighting was nearest.

Fleet foot on the correi,[2]
   Sage counsel in cumber,[3]
Red hand in the foray,
   How sound is thy slumber!
Like the dew on the mountain,
   Like the foam on the river,
Like the bubble on the fountain,
   Thou art gone, and for ever.

                                 Sir Walter Scott

[1] *Dirge, lament*
[2] *Vast hill-hollow*
[3] *Danger or defeat*

THE DAY OF BATTLE

"Far I hear the bugle blow
 To call me where I would not go,
And the guns begin the song,
'Soldier, fly or stay for long.'

"Comrade, if to turn and fly
 Made a soldier never die,
Fly I would, for who would not?
'Tis sure no pleasure to be shot.

"But since a man that runs away
Lives to die another day,
And cowards' funerals, when they come,
Are not wept so well at home.

"Therefore, though the best is bad,
Stand and do the best, my lad,
Stand and fight and see your slain
And take the bullet in your brain."

A. E. Housman

DECORATING THE SOLDIERS' GRAVES

A silent bivouac of the dead, we say,
    While on the low green tents we lay our flowers,
And with soft tread we take our reverent way
    Past where each seems to sleep away the hours.

A *silent* bivouac? Nay, they sleep not here:
    They have passed on; and, gleaming bright ahead,
Their camp-fires on yon heights of truth appear,
    Lighting the way that coming feet shall tread.

Their shot-torn flags still wave upon the air,
    There where some new heroic deed is done;
And, echoing loud, their shout still ringeth where
    Some new field waits, by brave hearts to be won.

The brave die never, though they sleep in dust:
    Their courage nerves a thousand living men,
Who seize and carry on the sacred trust,
    And win their noble victories o'er again.

Their graves are cradles of the purpose high
    That led them on the weary march, and through
The battles where the dying do not die,
    But live forever in the deeds they do.

And from these cradles rise the coming years,—
    The dead souls resurrected,—still to keep
The memory of those times of blood and tears,
    And carry on the work of those who sleep.

And thus the silent bivouac of the dead
    Finds voice, and thrills with throbbing life today;
And we, who softly by their green tents tread,
    Will hear and heed the noble words they say.

Minot J. Savage

DECORATION
Manibus date lilia plenis [1]

'Mid the flower-wreathed tombs I stand,
Bearing lilies in my hand.
Comrades! in what soldier-grave
Sleeps the bravest of the brave?

Is it he who sank to rest
With his colors round his breast?
Friendship makes his tomb a shrine,
Garlands veil it; ask not mine.

One low grave, yon trees beneath,
Bears no roses, wears no wreath;
Yet no heart more high and warm
Ever dared the battle-storm.

260

MEMORIAL DAY

Never gleamed a prouder eye
In the front of victory;
Never foot had firmer tread
On the field where hope lay dead,

Than are hid within this tomb,
Where the untended grasses bloom;
And no stone with feigned distress,
Mocks the sacred loneliness.

Youth and beauty, dauntless will,
Dreams that life could ne'er fulfil
Here lie buried,—here in peace
Wrongs and woes have found release.

Turning from my comrades' eyes,
Kneeling where a woman lies,
I strew lilies on the grave
Of the bravest of the brave.

Thomas Wentworth Higginson

[1] *Strew lilies with generous hands.*

DECORATION DAY

From many a field with patriot blood imbrued,
    From many a scene of suffering and despond,
    From many a dark ravine and rushy pond,
From many a wilderness and solitude,

From many a wreck in ocean caverns strewed,
   From many a stately tomb and lowly mound,
   The spirits of the slaughtered brave respond,
The martyrs of that host, in civil feud,

Which staked for Union lives and all. They leapt
   To save the Constitution and the State;
     They fought for liberty and right; they died,
Unselfishly, in Freedom's cause. Men wept,
   To see such sacrifice, though love so great,
     Such deeds of valor, swelled their hearts with
      pride.

               George Hurlbut Barbour

DECORATION DAY

   Earth from her winter slumber breaks;
   The morning of the year awakes.
   The vital warmth that buried lay
   Transcends again its house of clay,
   And to the greeting of the skies
   With thrilling harmony replies.

   A promise breathes from every furrow:
   "Dark yesterday makes bright to-morrow.
   Pursue no more the midnight oil;
   The sunlight measures cheer and toil;

MEMORIAL DAY

The winds proclaim, with odorous breath,
The life that triumphs over death."

Yet vanished days of many a year
Remain to us possessions dear;
We call the roll of those who dared;
We bless the saints who hardly fared,
Lending their martyred flesh to be
The torchlight of Truth's victory.

Still may we utter solemn praise
Of those whose prowess filled their days
With thoughts and deeds of high renown,
Which now our floral offerings crown.
But as our earth from south to north
Her glorious promise blazons forth,
And timid spring and summer bold
On autumn pour their wealth of gold,

So let our buried heroes live
In hands that freely guard and give,
In minds that, watchful, entertain
Great thoughts of Justice and her reign,
That tend, all other tasks above,
The household fires of faith and love,
And keep our banner, wide unfurled,
A pledge of blessing to the world.

Julia Ward Howe

Included by permission of, and by special arrangement with, Houghton Mifflin Company, the authorized publishers.

263

DECORATION DAY

Sleep, comrades, sleep and rest
    On this Field of the Grounded Arms,
Where foes no more molest,
    Nor sentry's shot alarms!

Ye have slept on the ground before,
    And started to your feet
At the cannon's sudden roar,
    Or the drum's redoubling beat.

But in this Camp of Death
    No sound your slumber breaks;
Here is no fevered breath,
    No wound that bleeds and aches.

All is repose and peace,
    Untrampled lies the sod;
The shouts of battle cease,
    It is the truce of God!

Rest, comrades, rest and sleep!
    The thoughts of men shall be
As sentinels to keep
    Your rest from danger free.

264

MEMORIAL DAY

Your silent tents of green
    We deck with fragrant flowers;
Yours has the suffering been,
    The memory shall be ours.

Henry Wadsworth Longfellow

Included by permission of, and by special arrangement with, Houghton Mifflin Company, the authorized publishers.

THE DUG-OUT

Why do you lie with your legs ungainly huddled,
And one arm bent across your sullen cold
Exhausted face? It hurts my heart to watch you,
Deep-shadowed from the candle's guttering gold;
And you wonder why I shake you by the shoulder;
Drowsy, you mumble and sigh and turn your head.
You are too young to fall asleep for ever;
And when you sleep you remind me of the dead.

Siegfried Sassoon

FLOWERS FOR THE BRAVE

Here bring your purple and gold,
    Glory of color and scent!
Scarlet of tulips bold,
    Buds blue as the firmament.

265

Hushed is the sound of the fife
    And the bugle piping clear;
The vivid and delicate life
    In the soul of the youthful year.

We bring to the quiet dead,
    With a gentle and tempered grief;
O'er the mounds so mute we shed
    The beauty of blossoms and leaf.

The flashing swords that were drawn
    No rust shall their fame destroy!
Boughs rosy as rifts of dawn,
    Like the blush on the cheek of joy.

Rich fires of the gardens and meads,
    We kindle these hearts above.
What splendor shall match their deeds;
    What sweetness can match our love?

Celia Thaxter

Included by permission of, and by special arrangement with, Houghton Mifflin Company, the authorized publishers.

THE HEROIC AGE

He speaks not well who doth his time deplore,
Naming it new and little and obscure,
Ignoble and unfit for lofty deeds.

MEMORIAL DAY

All times were modern in the time of them,
And this no more than others. Do thy part
Here in the living day, as did the great
Who made old days immortal! So shall men,
Gazing long back to this far-looming hour,
Say: "Then the time when men were truly men:
Tho' wars grew less, their spirits met the test
Of new conditions; conquering civic wrong;
Saving the state anew by virtuous lives;
Guarding the country's honor as their own,
And their own as their country's and their sons':
Proclaiming service the one test of worth;
Defying leaguèd fraud with single truth;
Knights of the spirit; warriors in the cause
Of justice absolute 'twixt man and man;
Not fearing loss; and daring to be pure.
When error through the land raged like a pest
They calmed the madness caught from mind to mind
By wisdom drawn from eld, and counsel sane;
And as the martyrs of the ancient world
Gave Death for man, so nobly gave they Life:
Those the great days, and that the heroic age."

Richard Watson Gilder

Included by permission of, and by special arrangement with, Houghton Mifflin Company, the authorized publishers.

JOHN BURNS OF GETTYSBURG

Have you heard the story that gossips tell
Of Burns of Gettysburg? No?   Ah, well:
Brief is the glory that hero earns,
Briefer the story of poor John Burns;
He was the fellow who won renown,—
The only man who didn't back down
When the rebels rode through his native town;
But held his own in the fight next day,
When all his townsfolk ran away.
That was in July, sixty-three,—
The very day that General Lee,
Flower of Southern chivalry,
Baffled and beaten, backward reeled
From a stubborn Meade and a barren field.

I might tell how, but the day before
John Burns stood at his cottage door,
Looking down the village street,
Where, in the shade of his peaceful vine,
He heard the low of his gathered kine,
And felt their breath with incense sweet;
Or, I might say, when the sunset burned
The old farm gable, he thought it turned
The milk that fell like a babbling flood
Into the milk-pail, red as blood;

MEMORIAL DAY

Or, how he fancied the hum of bees
Were bullets buzzing among the trees.
But all such fanciful thoughts as these
Were strange to a practical man like Burns,
Who minded only his own concerns,
Troubled no more by fancies fine
Than one of his calm-eyed, long-tailed kine,—
Quite old-fashioned and matter-of-fact,
Slow to argue, but quick to act.
That was the reason, as some folk say,
He fought so well on that terrible day.

And it was terrible. On the right
Raged for hours the heady fight,
Thundered the battery's double bass,—
Difficult music for men to face;
While on the left,—where now the graves
Undulate like the living waves
That all the day unceasing swept
Up to the pits the rebels kept,—
Round-shot ploughed the upland glades,
Sown with bullets, reaped with blades;
Shattered fences here and there,
Tossed their splinters in the air;
The very trees were stripped and bare;
The barns that once held yellow grain
Were heaped with harvests of the slain;
The cattle bellowed on the plain,

The turkeys screamed with might and main,
And brooding barn-fowl left their rest
With strange shells bursting in each nest.

Just where the tide of battle turns,
Erect and lonely, stood old John Burns.
How do you think the man was dressed?
He wore an ancient, long buff vest,
Yellow as saffron,—but his best;
And buttoned over his manly breast
Was a bright blue coat with a rolling collar,
And large gilt buttons,—size of a dollar,—
With tails that the country-folk called
    "swaller."
He wore a broad-brimmed, bell-crowned hat,
White as the locks on which it sat.
Never had such a sight been seen
For forty years on the village green,
Since old John Burns was a country beau,
And went to the "quiltings" long ago.

Close at his elbows all that day,
Veterans of the Peninsula,
Sunburnt and bearded, charged away;
And striplings, downy of lip and chin,—
Clerks that the Home-guard mustered in,—
Glanced, as they passed, at the hat he wore,
Then at the rifle his right hand bore;

And hailed him, from out their youthful lore,
With scraps of a slangy repertoire:
"How are you, White Hat?" "Put her
    through!"
"Your head's level!" and "Bully for you!"
Called him "Daddy,"—begged he'd disclose
The name of the tailor who made his clothes,
And what was the value he set on those;
While Burns, unmindful of jeer and scoff,
Stood there picking the rebels off,—
With his long brown rifle, and bell-crowned hat,
And the swallow-tails they were laughing at.

'Twas but a moment, for that respect
Which clothes all courage their voices checked;
And something the wildest could understand
Spake in the old man's strong right hand,
And his corded throat, and the lurking frown
Of his eyebrows under his old bell-crown;
Until, as they gazed, there crept an awe
Through the ranks in whispers, and some men saw
In the antique vestments and long white hair,
The Past of the Nation in battle there;
And some of the soldiers since declare
That the gleam of his old white hat afar,
Like the crested plume of the brave Navarre,
That day was their oriflamme of war.
Thus raged the battle.   You know the rest;

271

How the rebels, beaten, and backward pressed,
Broke at the final charge and ran.
At which John Burns,—a practical man—
Shouldered his rifle, unbent his brows,
And then went back to his bees and cows.
That is the story of old John Burns;
This is the moral the reader learns:
In fighting the battle, the question's whether
You'll show a hat that's white, or a feather.

Bret Harte

Included by permission of, and by special arrangement with, Houghton Mifflin Company, the authorized publishers.

KILLED AT THE FORD

He is dead, the beautiful youth,
The heart of honor, the tongue of truth,
He, the life and light of us all,
Whose voice was blithe as a bugle-call,
Whom all eyes followed with one consent,
The cheer of whose laugh, and whose pleasant word,
Hushed all murmurs of discontent.

Only last night, as we rode along,
Down the dark of the mountain gap,
To visit the picket-guard at the ford,

MEMORIAL DAY

Little dreaming of any mishap,
He was humming the words of some old song:
"Two red roses he had on his cap
And another he bore at the point of his sword."

Sudden and swift a whistling ball
Came out of a wood, and the voice was still;
Something I heard in the darkness fall,
And for a moment my blood grew chill;
I spake in a whisper, as he who speaks
In a room where some one is lying dead;
But he made no answer to what I said.

We lifted him up to his saddle again,
And through the mire and the mist and the rain
Carried him back to the silent camp,
And laid him as if asleep on his bed;
And I saw by the light of the surgeon's lamp
Two white roses upon his cheeks,
And one, just over his heart, blood-red!

And I saw in a vision how far and fleet
That fatal bullet went speeding forth,
Till it reached a town in the distant North,
Till it reached a house in a sunny street,
Till it reached a heart that ceased to beat
Without a murmur, without a cry;

And a bell was tolled in that far-off town,
For one who had passed from cross to crown,
And the neighbors wondered that she should die.

Henry Wadsworth Longfellow

*Included by permission of, and by special arrangement with, Houghton
Mifflin Company, the authorized publishers.*

A LAMENTATION

All looks be pale, hearts cold as stone,
For Hally now is dead and gone.
    Hally in whose sight,
        Most sweet sight,
All the earth late took delight.
    Every eye, weep with me,
    Joys drowned in tears must be.

His ivory skin, his comely hair,
His rosy cheeks so clear and fair,
    Eyes that once did grace
        His bright face,
Now in him all want their place.
    Eyes and hearts, weep with me.
    For who so kind as he?

His youth was like an April flower,
Adorned with beauty, love, and power.

274

MEMORIAL DAY

Glory strewed his way,
Whose wreaths gay
Now are all turnéd to decay.
Then, again, weep with me,
None feel more cause than we.

No more may his wished sight return.
His golden lamp no more can burn,
Quenched is all his flame,
His hoped fame
Now hath left him nought but name.
For him all weep with me,
Since more him none shall see.

Thomas Campion

LET WAR'S TEMPESTS CEASE

Lord, let war's tempests cease,
Fold the whole world in peace
Under Thy wings.
Make all the nations one,
All hearts beneath the sun,
Till Thou shalt reign alone,
Great King of Kings.

Henry Wadsworth Longfellow

Included by permission of, and by special arrangement with, Houghton Mifflin Company, the authorized publishers.

THE MARCH

I heard a voice that cried, "Make way for those who
    died!"
And all the colored crowd like ghosts at morning fled;
And down the waiting road, rank after rank there
    strode
In mute and measured march a hundred thousand
    dead.

A hundred thousand dead, with firm and noiseless
        tread,
All shadowy-gray yet solid, with faces gray and ghast,
And by the house they went, and all their brows were
    bent
Straight forward; and they passed, and passed, and
    passed, and passed,

But O there came a place, and O there came a face,
That clenched my heart to see it, and sudden turned
    my way;
And in the face that turned I saw two eyes that burned,
Never-forgotten eyes, and they had things to say.

Like desolate stars they shone one moment, and were
    gone,

MEMORIAL   DAY

And I sank down and put my arms across my head,
And felt them moving past, nor looked to see the last,
In steady silent march, our hundred thousand dead.

John C. Squire

Included by permission of the author and George H. Doran Company.

MEMORIAL DAY

A handful of old men walking down the village
    street
    In worn, brushed uniforms, their gray heads high;
A faded flag above them, one drum to lift their feet—
    *Look again, O heart of mine, and see what
    passes by!*

There's a vast crowd swaying, there's a wild band
    playing,
    The streets are full of marching men, of tramping
    cavalry.
Alive and young and straight again, they ride to greet
    a mate again—
    The gallant souls, the great souls that live
    eternally!

A handful of old men walking down the highways?
    Nay, we look on heroes that march among their
    peers,

The great, glad Companies have swung from heaven's
    byways
    And come to join their own again across the dusty
    years.

There are strong hands meeting, there are staunch
    hearts greeting—
A crying of remembered names, of deeds that shall
    not die.
A handful of old men?—Nay, my heart, look well
    again;
    The spirit of America today is marching by!

Theodosia Garrison

From "As the Larks Rise," by Theodosia Garrison.
Included by permission of G. P. Putnam's Sons.

MEMORIAL DAY

She saw the bayonets flashing in the sun,
  The flags that proudly waved; she heard the bugles
    calling;
She saw the tattered banners falling
About the broken staffs, as one by one
The remnant of the mighty army past;
And at the last
Flowers for the graves of those whose fight was done.

MEMORIAL   DAY

She heard the tramping of ten thousand feet
As the long line swept round the crowded square;
She heard the incessant hum
That filled the warm and blossom-scented air—
The shrilling fife, the roll and throb of drum,
The happy laugh, the cheer.   O, glorious and meet
To honor thus the dead,
Who chose the better part,
Who for their country bled!
—The dead! Great God! she stood there in the street,
Living, yet dead in soul and mind and heart—
While far away
His grave was deckt with flowers by strangers' hands
    to-day.

Richard Watson Gilder

*Included by permission of, and by special arrangement with, Houghton
Mifflin Company, the authorized publishers.*

MEMORIAL DAY

Is it enough to think to-day
Of all our brave, then put away
The thought until a year has sped?
Is this full honor for our dead?

Is it enough to sing a song
And deck a grave; and all year long
Forget the brave who died that we
Might keep our great land proud and free?

Full service needs a greater toll—
That we who live give heart and soul
To keep the land they died to save,
And be ourselves, in turn, the brave!

Annette Wynne

*Reprinted by permission from "For Days and Days," by Annette Wynne.
Copyright, 1919, by Frederick A. Stokes Company.*

THE MESSAGES

"I cannot quite remember . . . There were five
Dropt dead beside me in the trench—and three
Whispered their dying messages to me . . . "

Back from the trenches, more dead than alive,
Stone-deaf and dazed, and with a broken knee,
He hobbled slowly, muttering vacantly:

"I cannot quite remember . . . There were five
Dropt dead beside me in the trench—and three
Whispered their dying messages to me. . . .

MEMORIAL DAY

"Their friends are waiting, wondering how they
    thrive—
Waiting a word in silence patiently . . .
But what they said, or who their friends may be

"I cannot quite remember . . . There were five
Dropt dead beside me in the trench—and three
Whispered their dying messages to me. . . ."

Wilfrid Wilson Gibson

From the "Poems" of Wilfrid Wilson Gibson.
Included by permission of The Macmillan Company.

NIGHT AT GETTYSBURG

By day Golgotha sleeps, but when night comes
The army rallies to the beating drums;
Columns are formed and banners wave
O'er armies summoned from the grave.

The wheat field waves with reddened grain
And the wounded wail and writhe in pain.
The hard-held Bloody Angle drips anew
And Pickett charges with a ghostly crew.

While where the road to the village turns
Stands the tall shadow of old John Burns!

Don C. Seitz

From "In Praise of War," by Don C. Seitz.
Included by permission of Harper & Brothers.

NO MORE THE THUNDER OF CANNON

No more the thunder of cannon,
　　No more the clashing of swords,
No more the rage of the contest,
　　Nor the rush of contending hordes;
But, instead, the glad reunion,
　　The clasping of friendly hands,
The song, for the shout of battle,
　　Heard over the waiting lands.

O brothers, to-night we greet you
　　With smiles, half sad, half gay—
For our thoughts are flying backward
　　To the years so far away—
When with you who were part of the conflict,
　　With us who remember it all,
Youth marched with his waving banner,
　　And his voice like a bugle call!

We would not turn back the dial,
　　Nor live over the past again;
We would not the path re-travel,
　　Nor barter the "now" for the "then."
Yet, oh, for the bounding pulses,
　　And the strength to do and dare,
When life was one grand endeavor,
　　And work clasped hands with prayer!

MEMORIAL DAY

But blessed are ye, O brothers,
  Who feel in your souls alway
The thrill of the stirring summons
  You heard but to obey;
Who, whether the years go swift,
  Or whether the years go slow,
Will wear in your hearts forever
  The glory of long ago!

Julia C. R. Dorr

Included by permission of Charles Scribner's Sons.

ODE FOR DECORATION DAY

Bring flowers, to strew again
With fragrant purple rain
Of lilacs, and of roses white and red,
The dwellings of our dead—our glorious dead!
Let the bells ring a solemn funeral chime,
And wild war-music bring anew the time
  When they who sleep beneath
  Were full of vigorous breath,
And in their lusty manhood sallied forth,
  Holding in strong right hand
  The fortunes of the land,
The pride and power and safety of the North!

It seems but yesterday
The long and proud array—
But yesterday when e'en the solid rock
Shook as with earthquake shock—
As North and South, like two huge icebergs, ground
Against each other with convulsive bound,
And the whole world stood still
    To view the mighty war,
    And hear the thunderous roar,
While sheeted lightnings wrapped each plain and hill.

Alas! how few came back
From battle and from wrack!
Alas! how many lie
Beneath a Southern sky,
Who never heard the fearful fight was done,
And all they fought for, won!
Sweeter, I think, their sleep,
More peaceful and more deep,
Could they but know their wounds were not in vain;
Could they but hear the grand triumphal strain,
And see their homes unmarred by hostile tread.
Ah! let us trust it is so with our dead—
That they the thrilling joy of triumph feel,
And in that joy disdain the foeman's steel.
We mourn for all, but each doth think of one
    More precious to the heart than aught beside—

MEMORIAL DAY

Some father, brother, husband, or some son,
    Who came not back, or, coming, sank and died;
In him the whole sad list is glorified!
"He fell 'fore Richmond, in the seven long days
    When battle raged from morn till blood-dewed
       eve,
And lies there," one pale widowed mourner says,
    And knows not most to triumph or to grieve.
"My boy fell at Fair Oaks," another sighs;
"And mine at Gettysburg," his neighbor cries,
    And that great name each sad-eyed listener thrills.
I think of one who vanished when the press
Of battle surged along the Wilderness,
    And mourned the North upon her thousand hills.
O gallant brothers of the generous South!
    Foes for a day, and brothers for all time,
I charge you by the memories of our youth,
    By Yorktown's field and Montezuma's clime,
Hold our dead sacred; let them quietly rest
In your unnumbered vales, where God thought best!
Your vines and flowers learned long since to forgive,
And o'er their graves a broidered mantle weave;
Be you as kind as they are, and the word
Shall reach the Northland with each summer bird,
And thoughts as sweet as summer shall awake
Responsive to your kindness, and shall make
Our peace the peace of brothers once again,
And banish utterly the days of pain.

And ye, O Northmen! be ye not outdone
    In generous thought and deed.
We all do need forgiveness, every one;
    And they that give shall find it in their need.
Spare of your flowers to deck the stranger's grave,
    Who died for a lost cause;
A soul more daring, resolute, and brave
    Ne'er won a world's applause!
(A brave man's hatred pauses at the tomb.)
For him some Southern home was robed in gloom,
Some wife or mother looked, with longing eyes,
Through the sad days and nights, with tears and sighs—
Hope slowly hardening into gaunt Despair.
Then let your foeman's grave remembrance share;
Pity a higher charm to Valor lends,
And in the realms of Sorrow all are friends.

Yes, bring fresh flowers, and strew the soldier's grave,
    Whether he proudly lies
    Beneath our Northern skies,
Or where the Southern palms their branches wave.
Let the bells toll, and wild war-music swell,
    And for one day the thought of all the past—
    Full of those memories vast—
Come back and haunt us with its mighty spell!
Bring flowers then, once again,
And strew with fragrant rain

Of lilacs, and of roses white and red,
The dwellings of our dead.

Henry Peterson

ODE RECITED AT THE HARVARD COMMEMORATION

I with uncovered head
Salute the sacred dead,
Who went, and who return not.—Say not so!
'Tis not the grapes of Canaan that repay,
But the high faith that failed not by the way;
Virtue treads paths that end not in the grave;
No ban of endless night exiles the brave;
And to the saner mind
We rather seem the dead that stayed behind.
Blow, trumpets, all your exultations blow!
For never shall their aureoled presence lack:
I see them muster in a gleaming row,
With ever-youthful brows that nobler show;
We find in our dull road their shining track;
In every nobler mood
We feel the orient of their spirit glow,
Part of our life's unalterable good,
Of all our saintlier aspiration;
They come transfigured back,
Secure from change in their high-hearted ways,

287

Beautiful evermore, and with the rays
Of morn on their white Shields of Expectation!

Bow down, dear Land, for thou hast found release!
    Thy God, in these distempered days,
    Hath taught thee the sure wisdom of His ways,
And through thine enemies hath wrought thy peace!
    Bow down in prayer and praise!
No poorest in thy borders but may now
Lift to the juster skies a man's enfranchised brow.
O Beautiful! my Country! ours once more!
Smoothing thy gold of war-dishevelled hair
O'er such sweet brows as never other wore,
    And letting thy set lips,
    Freed from wrath's pale eclipse,
The rosy edges of their smile lay bare,
What words divine of lover or of poet
Could tell our love and make thee know it,
Among the Nations bright beyond compare?
    What were our lives without thee?
    What all our lives to save thee?
    We reck not what we gave thee;
    We will not dare to doubt thee,
But ask whatever else, and we will dare!

James Russell Lowell

(*Selected*)

Included by permission of, and by special arrangement with, Houghton Mifflin Company, the authorized publishers.

OUR NATION FOREVER

*Sung at a Union Concert of Northern and Southern
Songs in the Chautauqua Amphitheatre,* 1883

Ring out to the stars the glad chorus!
  Let bells in sweet melody chime;
Ring out to the sky bending o'er us
  The chant of a nation sublime:
One land with a history glorious!
One God and one faith all victorious!

The songs of the camp-fires are blended,
  The North and the South are no more;
The conflict forever is ended,
  From the lakes to the palm-girded shore.

One people united forever
  In hope greets the promising years;
No discord again can dissever
  A Union cemented by tears.

The past shall retain but one story—
  A record of courage and love;
The future shall cherish one glory,
  While the stars shine responsive above.

With emotions of pride and of sorrow,
  Bring roses and lilies to-day;

In the dawn of the nation's to-morrow
　　We garland the blue and the gray.
One land with a history glorious!
One God and one faith all victorious!

Wallace Bruce

From "Old Homestead Poems," by Wallace Bruce.
Included by permission of Harper & Brothers.

OVER THEIR GRAVES

Over their graves rang once the bugle call,
The searching shrapnel and the crashing ball;
　　The shriek, the shock of battle, and the neigh
　　Of horse; the cries of anguish and dismay;
And the loud cannon's thunders that appall.

Now through the years the brown pine-needles fall,
The vines run riot by the old stone wall,
　　By hedge, by meadow streamlet, far away,
　　　　Over their graves.

We love our dead where'er so held in thrall.
Than they no Greek more bravely died, nor Gaul—
　　A love that's deathless!—but they look today
　　With no reproaches on us when we say,
"Come, let us clasp your hands, we're brothers all,
　　　　Over their graves!"

Henry J. Stockard

290

REQUIEM

When the last voyage is ended,
    And the last sail is furled,
When the last blast is weathered,
    And the last bolt is hurled,
      And there comes no more the sound of the old
        ship bell—
      Sailor, sleep well!

When the last Post is blown,
    And the last volley fired,
When the last sod is thrown,
    And the last Foe retired,
      And thy last bivouac is made under the ground—
      Soldier, sleep sound!

Joseph Lee

REQUIEM FOR A YOUNG SOLDIER

Peace to-night, heroic spirit!
    Pain is overpast.
All the strife with life is ended;
    You may rest at last.

The devotion that, amazing,
    Welled from out the deep
Of your being, no more needed,
    Quiet you may sleep:

291

Sleep, who, giving all for others,
  Battled till the victory nigh,
You, too, toil and heart-break over,
  Had the right to die! . . .

We may guard the grave that holds you,
  As a shrine of Truth
Lighted by the pure devotion
  Of your radiant youth;

We, you died for, may forget you!
  You will have no care,
Who, content, to-night are sleeping—
  Painless, dreamless, there!

                    Florence Earle Coates

Included by permission of, and by special arrangement with, Houghton
Mifflin Company, the authorized publishers.

REQUIESCANT

In lonely watches night by night
Great visions burst upon my sight,
For down the stretches of the sky
The hosts of dead go marching by.

Strange ghostly banners o'er them float,
Strange bugles sound an awful note,
And all their faces and their eyes
Are lit with starlight from the skies.

MEMORIAL DAY

The anguish and the pain have passed
And peace hath come to them at last,
But in the stern looks linger still
The iron purpose and the will.

Dear Christ, who reign'st above the flood
Of human tears and human blood,
A weary road these men have trod,
O house them in the home of God!

Frederick George Scott

Included by permission of the author and of Constable and Company, Limited.

THE REVEILLE

Hark! I hear the tramp of thousands,
    And of armed men the hum;
Lo! a nation's hosts have gathered
    Round the quick alarming drum,—
        Saying, "Come,
        Freemen, come!
Ere your heritage be wasted," said the quick alarming
                drum.

"Let me of my heart take counsel;
    War is not of life the sum.
Who shall stay and reap the harvest

When the autumn days shall come?"
    But the drum
    Echoed, "Come!
Death shall reap the braver harvest," said the solemn-
    sounding drum.

"But when won the coming battle,
    What of profit springs therefrom?
What if conquest, subjugation,
    Even greater ills become?"
      But the drum
      Answered, "Come!
You must do the sum to prove it," said the Yankee
    answering drum.

Thus they answered,—hoping, fearing,
    Some in faith, and doubting some,
Till a trumpet-voice, proclaiming,
    Said, "My chosen people, come!"
      Then the drum,
      Lo! was dumb,
For the great heart of the nation, throbbing, answered,
    "Lord, we come!"

Bret Harte

Included by permission of, and by special arrangement with, Houghton Mifflin Company, the authorized publishers.

ROLL-CALL

"Corporal Green!" the orderly cried;
  "Here!" was the answer loud and clear,
    From the lips of a soldier who stood near,—
And "Here!" was the word the next replied.

"Cyrus Drew!"—then a silence fell;
  This time no answer followed the call;
  Only his rear-man had seen him fall:
Killed or wounded—he could not tell.

There they stood in the failing light,
  These men of battle with grave, dark looks,
  As plain to be read as open books,
While slowly gathered the shades of night.

The fern on the hillsides were splashed with blood,
  And down in the corn, where the poppies grew,
  Were redder stains than the poppies knew,
And crimson-dyed was the river's flood.

For the foe had crossed from the other side,
  That day, in the face of a murderous fire
  That swept them down in its terrible ire;
And their life-blood went to color the tide.

"Herbert Cline!"—At the call there came
  Two stalwart soldiers into the line,
  Bearing between them this Herbert Cline,
Wounded and bleeding to answer his name.

"Ezra Kerr!"—and a voice answered "Here!"
  "Hiram Kerr!"—but no man replied.
    They were brothers, these two; the sad wind
      sighed,
And a shudder crept through the cornfield near.

"Ephraim Deane!"—then a soldier spoke:
  "Deane carried our regiment's colors," he said,
  "When our ensign was shot; I left him dead
Just after the enemy wavered and broke.

"Close by the roadside his body lies;
  I paused a moment and gave him to drink;
  He murmured his mother's name, I think,
And Death came with it and closed his eyes."

'Twas a victory—yes; but it cost us dear:
  For that company's roll, when called at night,
  Of a hundred men who went into the fight,
Numbered but twenty that answered "*Here!*"

Nathaniel Graham Shepherd

SHERIDAN'S RIDE

Up from the south, at break of day,
Bringing to Winchester fresh dismay,
The affrighted air with a shudder bore,
Like a herald in haste to the chieftain's door,
The terrible grumble, and rumble, and roar,
Telling the battle was on once more,
    And Sheridan twenty miles away.

And wider still those billows of war
Thunder'd along the horizon's bar;
And louder yet into Winchester roll'd
The roar of that red sea uncontroll'd,
Making the blood of the listener cold,
As he thought of the stake in that fiery fray,
    With Sheridan twenty miles away.

But there is a road from Winchester town,
A good broad highway leading down:
And there, through the flush of the morning light,
A steed as black as the steeds of night
Was seen to pass, as with eagle flight,
As if he knew the terrible need,
He stretch'd away with his utmost speed;
Hills rose and fell; but his heart was gay,
    With Sheridan fifteen miles away.

Still sprang from those swift hoofs, thundering south,
The dust like smoke from the cannon's mouth,
Or the trail of a comet, sweeping faster and faster,
Foreboding to traitors the doom of disaster.
The heart of the steed and the heart of the master
Were beating like prisoners assaulting their walls,
Impatient to be where the battle-field calls;
Every nerve of the charger was strained to full play,
    With Sheridan only ten miles away.

Under his spurring feet, the road
Like an arrowy Alpine river flow'd,
And the landscape sped away behind
Like an ocean flying before the wind;
And the steed, like a bark fed with furnace ire,
Swept on, with his wild eye full of fire.
But, lo! he is nearing his heart's desire;
He is snuffing the smoke of the rearing fray,
    With Sheridan only five miles away.

The first that the general saw were the groups
Of stragglers, and then the retreating troops;
What was done? what to do? a glance told him both.
Then striking his spurs with a terrible oath,
He dash'd down the line, 'mid a storm of huzzas,
And the wave of retreat checked its course there,
    because

MEMORIAL DAY

The sight of the master compell'd it to pause.
With foam and with dust the black charger was gray;
By the flash of his eye, and the red nostril's play,
He seem'd to the whole great army to say:
"I have brought you Sheridan all the way
       From Winchester down to save the day."

Hurrah! hurrah for Sheridan!
Hurrah! hurrah for horse and man!
And when their statues are placed on high,
Under the dome of the Union sky,
The American soldier's Temple of Fame,
There with the glorious general's name
Be it said, in letters both bold and bright:
       "Here is the steed that saved the day
By carrying Sheridan into the fight,
       From Winchester,—twenty miles away!"

                                 Thomas Buchanan Read

THE SLEEP OF THE BRAVE

How sleep the brave, who sink to rest,
By all their country's wishes blessed!
When Spring, with dewy fingers cold,
Returns to deck their hallowed mold,
She there shall dress a sweeter sod
Than Fancy's feet have ever trod.

By fairy hands their knell is rung;
By forms unseen their dirge is sung;
There Honor comes, a pilgrim gray,
To bless the turf that wraps their clay;
And Freedom shall awhile repair,
To dwell a weeping hermit there!

William Collins

THE SOLDIER'S GRAVE

Strew lightly o'er the soldier's grave
    The springtime blossoms fresh and white,
    And deck with wreaths and garlands bright
The silent couches of the brave.

They fought—they died—they lie at rest
    Beneath yon low and grassy mounds;
    No more for them the trumpet sounds
To thrill the patriotic breast.

But though they mingle with the dust
    In that dark kingdom, where Decay
    Sits thronéd in his halls of clay,
Their memory is free from rust.

For well we love to honor those
    Who bravely fell amid the fight,
    Who sank in all their vanquished might
Upon the field among their foes.

MEMORIAL DAY

We honor both—the blue, the gray—
    For time hath blotted from the mind
    All bitter thoughts and words unkind
And washed all prejudice away.

And we remember only this,—
    They bravely fought—they bravely died;
    And, hero-like, their souls should ride
Along the ether seas of bliss.

Then spread upon each grave today
    The fragrant blossoms of the spring,
    And simple wreaths and garlands fling
Above the soldier's honored clay.

                Henry D. Muir

SONG FOR MEMORIAL DAY

Let us to-day,
Who breathe the final sweetness of the May,
Bring the enwreathéd bay
For those who trod the sacrificial way!
O sacred sod,
And O endearéd dust,
Thus would we keep our trust,—
Our trust which is remembrance, and the just
Tribute to those who fought and found their God!

Not with Love's melting eyes
Bending above them did they drop the mould
Of their mortality, and watch unfold
The bright celestial skies;
The face they saw
Was red-envisaged Battle, with the awe
Of thunders round about him wide unrolled;
Not upon fair white wings, but wings of flame,
The summoning vision came.

In many a garden-close
The year's first rose
Opens its perfumed petals to the day;
Then twine these with the bay,
These tokens redolent, that they may be
As fires about the shrine of Memory,
Making perennially sweet the airs
Whereon are borne our prayers!
Our prayers!—Yea, let us lift them! Those that sleep
Have won the last great conflict, gained the crown
Of radiance and renown,
Leaving us warders of their heritage;
Be our beseechment, then, that we may keep
The land for which they bled
(Loyal and laureled dead!)
Unsullied as their courage, a white light

Of peace and purity in all men's sight
For the unfolding age!

Clinton Scollard

Included by permission of the author.

SPRING IN WAR-TIME

I feel the spring far off, far off,
    The faint, far scent of bud and leaf—
Oh, how can spring take heart to come
    To a world in grief,
    Deep grief?

The sun turns north, the days grow long,
    Later the evening star grows bright—
How can the daylight linger on
    For men to fight,
    Still fight?

The grass is waking in the ground,
    Soon it will rise and blow in waves—
How can it have the heart to sway
    Over the graves,
    New graves?

Under the boughs where lovers walked
    The apple-blooms will shed their breath—

But what of all the lovers now
    Parted by Death,
    Grey Death?

Sara Teasdale

From "Rivers to the Sea," by Sara Teasdale.
Included by permission of The Macmillan Company.

STANZAS ON FREEDOM

Men! whose boast it is that ye
Come of fathers brave and free,
If there breathe on earth a slave,
Are ye truly free and brave?
If ye do not feel the chain,
When it works a brother's pain,
Are ye not base slaves indeed,
Slaves unworthy to be freed?

Women! who shall one day bear
Sons to breathe New England air,
If ye hear, without a blush,
Deeds to make the roused blood rush
Like red lava through your veins,
For your sisters now in chains—
Answer! are ye fit to be
Mothers of the brave and free?

MEMORIAL DAY

Is true Freedom but to break
Fetters for our own dear sake,
And, with leathern hearts, forget
That we owe mankind a debt?
No! true freedom is to share
All the chains our brothers wear,
And, with heart and hand, to be
Earnest to make others free!

They are slaves who fear to speak
For the fallen and the weak;
They are slaves who will not choose
Hatred, scoffing, and abuse,
Rather than in silence shrink
From the truth they needs must think;
They are slaves who dare not be
In the right with two or three.

James Russell Lowell

*Included by permission of, and by special arrangement with, Houghton,
Mifflin Company, the authorized publishers.*

TAPS

Sleep
Now the charge is won,
Sleep in the narrow clod;
Now it is set of sun,
Sleep till the trump of God.
Sleep.

Sleep.
Fame is a bugle call
Blown past a crumbling wall,
Battles are clean forgot,
Captains and towns are not,
Sleep shall outlast them all.
Sleep.

Lizette Woodworth Reese

Included by permission of the Estate of Thomas B. Mosher.

THE TROOP OF THE GUARD

There's a tramping of hoofs in the busy street,
    There's clanking of sabres on floor and stair,
There's sound of restless, hurrying feet,
Of voices that whisper, of lips that entreat,—
    Will they live, will they die, will they strive, will
        they dare?—
The houses are garlanded, flags flutter gay,
For a troop of the Guard rides forth to-day.

Oh, the troopers will ride and their hearts will leap,
    When it's shoulder to shoulder and friend to friend-
But it's some to the pinnacle, some to the deep,
And some in the glow of their strength to sleep,
    And for all it's a fight to the tale's far end.
And it's each to his goal, nor turn nor sway,
When the troop of the Guard rides forth to-day.

MEMORIAL DAY

The dawn is upon us, the pale light speeds
    To the Zenith with glamor and golden dart.
On, up! Boot and saddle! Give spurs to your steeds!
There's a city beleaguered that cries for men's deeds,
    With the pain of the world in its cavernous heart.
        Ours be the triumph! Humanity calls!
          Life's not a dream in the clover!
      On to the walls, on to the walls,
        On to the walls, and over!

    The wine is spent, the tale is spun,
    The revelry of youth is done.
    The horses prance, the bridles clink,
    While maidens fair in bright array
    With us the last sweet goblet drink,
    Then bid us, 'Mount and ride away!'
    Into the dawn we ride, we ride,
    Fellow and fellow, side by side;
    Galloping over the field and hill,
    Over the marshland, stalwart still,
    Into the forest's shadowy hush
    Where spectres walk in sunless day,
    And in dark pool and branch and bush
    The treacherous Will o' the Wisp lights play.
    Out of the wood 'neath the risen sun,
    Weary we gallop, one by one,
    To a richer hope and a stronger foe
    And a hotter fight in the fields below—

Each man his own slave, each his lord,
For the golden spurs and the victor's sword!

. . . . . .

The portals are open, the white road leads
  Through wicket and garden, o'er stone and sod.
On, up! Boot and saddle! Give spurs to your steeds!
There's a city beleaguered that cries for men's deeds,
  For the faith that is strength and the love that is
    God.
      On through the dawning! Humanity calls!
        Life's not a dream in the clover.
      On to the walls, on to the walls,
        On to the walls, and over!

Hermann Hagedorn

Included by permission of the author.

THE TRUMPET

Rise up, rise up,
And, as the trumpet blowing
Chases the dreams of men,
As the dawn glowing
The stars that left unlit
The land and water,
Rise up and scatter
The dew that covers
The print of last night's lovers—
Scatter it, scatter it!

MEMORIAL DAY

While you are listening
To the clear horn,
Forget, men, everything
On this earth newborn,
Except that it is lovelier
Than any mysteries.
Open your eyes to the air
 That has washed the eyes of the stars
Through all the dewy night:
Up with the light,
To the old wars;
Arise, arise!

Edward Thomas

Included by permission of Henry Holt and Company.

UNDER THE STARS

*Tell me what sail the seas
    Under the stars?*
Ships, and ships' companies
    Off to the wars.

Steel are the ships' great sides,
    Steel every gun,
Backward they thrust the tides,
    Swiftly they run.

Steel is the sailor's heart,
    Stalwart his arm,
His the Republic's part
    Thro' cloud and storm.

Tell me what colors there
    Stream from the spars?
Red stripes and white they bear,
    Blue, with bright stars:

Red for brave hearts that burn
    With liberty,
White for the peace they earn
    Making men free,

Stars for the Heaven above,
    Blue for the deep—
Where in their country's love
    Heroes shall sleep.

Tell me why on the breeze
    These banners blow?
Ships, and ships' companies,
    Eagerly go

Warring, like all our line,
    Freedom to friend,
Under this starry sign
    True to the end.

MEMORIAL DAY

Fair is the Flag's renown,
    Sacred her scars,
Sweet the death she shall crown
    Under the stars.

Wallace Rice

Included by permission of the author.

VALLEY OF THE SHADOW

God, I am travelling out to death's sea,
    I, who exulted in sunshine and laughter,
Thought not of dying—death is such waste of me!
    Grant me one comfort: Leave not the hereafter
Of mankind to war, as though I had died not—
    I, who in battle, my comrade's arm linking,
Shouted and sang—life in my pulses hot,
    Throbbing and dancing! Let not my sinking
In dark be for naught, my death a vain thing!
    God, let me know it the end of man's fever!
Make my last breath a bugle call, carrying
    Peace o'er the valleys and cold hills, for ever!

John Galsworthy

Included by permission of Charles Scribner's Sons.

A WAR SONG

Prepare, prepare the iron helm of War,
Bring forth the lots, cast in the spacious orb;
The Angel of Fate turns them with mighty hands,

311

And casts them out upon the darkened earth!
          Prepare, prepare!

Prepare your hearts for Death's cold hand! prepare
Your souls for flight, your bodies for the earth;
Prepare your arms for glorious victory;
Prepare your eyes to meet a holy God!
          Prepare, prepare!

Whose fatal scroll is that? Methinks 'tis mine!
Why sinks my heart, why faltereth my tongue?
Had I three lives, I'd die in such a cause,
And rise, with ghosts, over the well-fought field.
          Prepare, prepare!

The arrows of Almighty God are drawn!
Angels of death stand in the lowering heavens!
Thousands of souls must seek the realms of light,
And walk together on the clouds of heaven!
          Prepare, prepare!

Soldiers, prepare! Our cause is Heaven's cause;
Soldiers, prepare! Be worthy of our cause:
Prepare to meet our fathers in the sky:
Prepare, O troops, that are to fall to-day!
          Prepare, prepare!

William Blake

From "*A War Song to Englishmen.*"

THANKSGIVING DAY IN POETRY

The good God bless this day,
And we forever and aye
      Keep our love living,
Till all men 'neath heaven's dome
Sing Freedom's Harvest-home
      In one Thanksgiving!

Robert Bridges

Included by permission of the author.

THE BEAUTIFUL WORLD

Here's a song of praise for a beautiful world,
For the banner of blue that's above it unfurled,
For the streams that sparkle and sing to the sea,
For the bloom in the glade and the leaf on the tree;
Here's a song of praise for a beautiful world.

Here's a song of praise for the mountain peak,
Where the wind and the lightning meet and speak,
For the golden star on the soft night's breast,
And the silvery moonlight's path to rest;
Here's a song of praise for a beautiful world.

Here's a song of praise for the rippling notes
That come from a thousand sweet bird throats,
For the ocean wave and the sunset glow,
And the waving fields where the reapers go;
Here's a song of praise for a beautiful world.

Here's a song of praise for the ones so true,
And the kindly deeds they have done for you;
For the great earth's heart, when it's understood,
Is struggling still toward the pure and good;
Here's a song of praise for a beautiful world.

Here's a song of praise for the One who guides,
For He holds the ships and He holds the tides,
And underneath and around and above.
The world is lapped in the light of His love;
Here's a song of praise for a beautiful world.

                                W. L. Childress

A CHILD'S THOUGHT OF HARVEST

Out in the fields which were green last May,
But are rough and stubbled and brown to-day,
They are stacking the sheaves of the yellow wheat,
And raking the aftermath dry and sweet,
The barley and oats and golden rye
Are safely stored in the granary;
Where the pumpkins border the tall corn rows,
The busy reaper comes and goes;
And only the apples set so thick
On the orchard boughs are left to pick.

What a little time it seems since May—
Not very much longer than yesterday!
Yet all this growing, which now is done
And finished, was scarcely then begun.
The nodding wheat and high, strong screen
Of corn were but little points of green.

THANKSGIVING   DAY

The apple blossoms were pink and sweet,
But no one could gather them to eat;
And all this food for hungry men
Was but buds or seeds just planted then.

Susan Coolidge

THE CHILD'S WORLD

Great, wide, beautiful, wonderful world,
With the wonderful water round you curled,
And the wonderful grass upon your breast,
World, you are beautifully drest.

The wonderful air is over me,
And the wonderful wind is shaking the tree—
It walks on the water, and whirls the mills,
And talks to itself on the top of the hills.

You friendly Earth, how far do you go,
With the wheat-fields that nod and the rivers that flow
With cities and gardens, and cliffs and isles,
And people upon you for thousands of miles?

Ah! you are so great, and I am so small,
I hardly can think of you, World, at all;
And yet, when I said my prayers to-day,
My mother kissed me, and said, quite gay,

"If the wonderful World is great to you,
And great to father and mother, too,
You are more than the Earth, though you are such a
     dot!
You can love and think, and the Earth cannot!"

William Brighty Rands

THE CORN-SONG

Heap high the farmer's wintry hoard!
    Heap high the golden corn!
No richer gift has Autumn poured
    From out her lavish horn!

Let other lands, exulting, glean
    The apple from the pine,
The orange from its glossy green,
    The cluster from the vine;

We better love the hardy gift
    Our rugged vales bestow,
To cheer us when the storm shall drift
    Our harvest-fields with snow.

Through vales of grass and meads of flowers
    Our ploughs their furrows made,
While on the hills the sun and showers
    Of changeful April played.

THANKSGIVING DAY

We dropped the seed o'er hill and plain
    Beneath the sun of May,
And frightened from our sprouting grain
    The robber crows away.

All through the long, bright days of June
    Its leaves grew green and fair,
And waved in hot midsummer's noon
    Its soft and yellow hair.

And now, with autumn's moonlit eves,
    Its harvest-time has come,
We pluck away the frosted leaves,
    And bear the treasure home.

There, when the snows about us drift,
    And winter winds are cold,
Fair hands the broken grain shall sift,
    And knead its meal of gold.

Let vapid idlers loll in silk
    Around their costly board;
Give us the bowl of samp and milk,
    By homespun beauty poured!

Where'er the wide old kitchen hearth
    Sends up its smoky curls,
Who will not thank the kindly earth,
    And bless our farmer girls!

Then shame on all the proud and vain,
    Whose folly laughs to scorn
The blessing of our hardy grain,
    Our wealth of golden corn!

Let earth withhold her goodly root,
    Let mildew blight the rye,
Give to the worm the orchard's fruit,
    The wheat-field to the fly:

But let the good old crop adorn
    The hills our fathers trod;
Still let us, for his golden corn,
    Send up our thanks to God!

                    John Greenleaf Whittier

Included by permission of Houghton Mifflin Company.

EVERY DAY THANKSGIVING DAY

Sweet it is to see the sun
    Shining on Thanksgiving Day,
Sweet it is to see the snow
    Fall as if it came to stay;
Sweet is everything that comes,
    For all makes cheer, Thanksgiving Day.

THANKSGIVING DAY

Fine is the pantry's goodly store,
    And fine the heaping dish and tray;
Fine the church-bells ringing; fine
    All the dinners' great array,
Things we'd hardly dare to touch,
    Were it not Thanksgiving Day.

Dear the people coming home,
    Dear glad faces long away,
Dear the merry cries, and dear
    All the glad and happy play.
Dear the thanks, too, that we give
    For all of this Thanksgiving Day.

But sweeter, finer, dearer far
    It well might be if on our way,
With love for all, with thanks to Heaven,
    We did not wait for time's delay,
But, with remembered blessings then
    Made every day Thanksgiving Day.

Harriet Prescott Spofford

THE FEAST-TIME OF THE YEAR

This is the feast-time of the year,
When plenty pours her wine of cheer,
And even humble boards may spare
To poorer poor a kindly share.

While bursting barns and granaries know
A richer, fuller overflow,
And they who dwell in golden ease
Bless without toil, yet toil to please.
This is the feast-time of the year,
The blessed advent draweth near;
Let rich and poor together break
The bread of love for Christ's sweet sake,
Against the time when rich and poor
Must ope for Him a common door,
Who comes a guest, yet makes a feast,
And bids the greatest and the least.

Anonymous

THE FIRST THANKSGIVING DAY

In Puritan New England a year had passed away
Since first beside the Plymouth coast the English
Mayflower lay,
When Bradford, the good Governor, sent fowlers forth
to snare
The turkey and the wild-fowl, to increase the scanty
fare:—

"Our husbandry hath prospered, there is corn enough
for food,
Though the peas be parched in blossom, and the grain
indifferent good.

322

Who blessed the loaves and fishes for the feast miracu-
 lous,
And filled the widow's cruse, He hath remembered us!

"Give thanks unto the Lord of Hosts, by whom we all
 are fed,
Who granted us our daily prayer, 'Give us our daily
 bread!'
By us and by our children let this day be kept for aye,
In memory of His bounty, as the land's Thanksgiving
 Day."

Each brought his share of Indian meal the pious feast
 to make,
With the fat deer from the forest and the wild fowl
 from the brake.
And chanted hymn and prayer were raised—though
 eyes with tears were dim—
"The Lord He hath remembered us, let us remember
 Him!"

Then Bradford stood up at their head and lifted up
 his voice:
"The corn is gathered from the field, I call you to
 rejoice;
Thank God for all His mercies, from the greatest to
 the least,
Together we have *fasted*, friends, together let us *feast*.

"The Lord who led forth Israel was with us in the
    waste:
Sometime in light, sometime in cloud, before us He
    hath paced;
Now give Him thanks, and pray to Him who holds us
    in His hand
To prosper us and make of this a strong and mighty
    land!"

From Plymouth to the Golden Gate to-day their
    children tread,
The mercies of that bounteous Hand upon the land are
    shed;
The "flocks are on a thousand hill," the prairies wave
    with grain,
The cities spring like mushrooms now where once was
    desert-plain.

Heap high the board with plenteous cheer and gather
    to the feast,
And toast that sturdy Pilgrim band whose courage
    never ceased.
Give praise to that All Gracious One by whom their
    steps were led,
And thanks unto the harvest's Lord who sends our
    "daily bread."

Alice Williams Brotherton
Included by permission of the author.

324

THANKSGIVING DAY

HARVEST HYMN

Once more the liberal year laughs out
 O'er richer stores than gems or gold;
Once more with harvest-song and shout
 Is Nature's bloodless triumph told.

Oh, favors every year made new!
 Oh, gifts with rain and sunshine sent!
The bounty overruns our due,
 The fulness shames our discontent.

We shut our eyes, the flowers bloom on;
 We murmur, but the corn-ears fill,
We choose the shadow, but the sun
 That casts it shines behind us still.

Who murmurs at his lot to-day?
 Who scorns his native fruit and bloom?
Or sighs for dainties far away,
 Beside the bounteous board of home?

Thank Heaven, instead, that Freedom's arm
 Can change a rocky soil to gold,—
That brave and generous lives can warm
 A clime with northern ices cold.

And let these altars, wreathed with flowers
   And piled with fruits, awake again
Thanksgivings for the golden hours,
   The early and the latter rain!

John Greenleaf Whittier

Included by permission of The Houghton Mifflin Company.

HYMN

*Written for the Two Hundredth Anniversary of the
Old South Church, Beverly, Massachusetts*

The sea sang sweetly to the shore
   Two hundred years ago:
To weary pilgrim-ears it bore
   A welcome, deep and low.

They gathered, in the autumnal calm,
   To their first house of prayer;
And softly rose their Sabbath psalm
   On the wild woodland air.

The ocean took the echo up;
   It rang from tree to tree:
And praise, as from an incense-cup,
   Poured over earth and sea.

THANKSGIVING DAY

They linger yet upon the breeze,
     The hymns our fathers sung:
They rustle in the roadside trees,
     And give each leaf a tongue.

The grand old sea is moaning yet
     With music's mighty pain:
No chorus has arisen, to fit
     Its wondrous anthem-strain.

When human hearts are tuned to Thine,
     Whose voice is in the sea,
Life's murmuring waves a song divine
     Shall chant, O God, to Thee!

Lucy Larcom

Included by permission of The Houghton Mifflin Company.

A HYMN OF THANKSGIVING
"Out of his Treasuries."—Psalms, cxxxv, 7.

Thou who art Lord of the wind and rain,
     Lord of the east and western skies
And of the hilltop and the plain
     And of the stars that sink and rise,
Keeper of Time's great mysteries
     That are but blindly understood—
Give us to know that all of these
     Labor together for our good.

OUR HOLIDAYS IN POETRY

Thou who must laugh at bounding line
    Setting the little lands apart;
Thou who hast given corn and wine
    Give to us each a thankful heart.
Show us the worth of wounds and scars,
    Show us the grace that grows of grief,
Thou who hast flung the racing stars;
    Thou who hast loosed the falling leaf.

Count us the treasures that we hold—
    Wonderful peace of the wintry lands,
All of the summer's beaten gold
    Poured in our eager, out-held hands;
Open the book of the rounded year
    Paged with our pleasures and our pains—
Show us the writings where appear
    Losses o'er-balanced by the gains.

Thou who art Lord of the sea and shore,
    Lord of the gates of Day and Night—
This have we had of Thy great store:
    Laughter and love, and life and light,
Sorrow and sweetness, smile and song—
    Blessings that blend in all of these—
Have them and hold them over-long,
    Out of Thy wondrous treasuries.

Wilbur Dick Nesbit

Included by permission of the author.

THE LANDING OF THE PILGRIM FATH-
ERS IN NEW ENGLAND

The breaking waves dashed high
    On a stern and rock-bound coast,
And the woods against a stormy sky
    Their giant branches tossed;

And the heavy night hung dark
    The hills and waters o'er,
When a band of exiles moored their bark
    On the wild New England shore.

Not as the conqueror comes,
    They, the true-hearted, came;
Not with the roll of the stirring drums,
    And the trumpet that sings of fame;

Not as the flying come,
    In silence and in fear;—
They shook the depths of the desert gloom
    With their hymns of lofty cheer.

Amidst the storm they sang,
    And the stars heard, and the sea;
And the sounding aisles of the dim woods rang
    To the anthem of the free!

OUR HOLIDAYS IN POETRY

The ocean eagle soared
    From his nest by the white wave's foam;
And the rocking pines of the forest roared—
    This was their welcome home!

There were men with hoary hair
    Amidst that pilgrim band;—
Why had they come to wither there,
    Away from their childhood's land?

There was woman's fearless eye,
    Lit by her deep love's truth;
There was manhood's brow, serenely high,
    And the fiery heart of youth.

What sought they thus afar?—
    Bright jewels of the mine?
The wealth of seas, the spoils of war?—
    They sought a faith's pure shrine!

Ay, call it holy ground,
    The soil where first they trod;
They have left unstained what there they found–
    Freedom to worship God.

Felicia Hemans

PILGRIM SONG

*Written for the Society of Mayflower Descendants in
the State of Pennsylvania*

Pilgrims of the trackless deep,
  Leaving all, our fathers came,
Life and liberty to keep
  In Jehovah's awful name.
Neither pillared flame nor cloud
  Made the wild, for them, rejoice
But their hearts, with sorrow bowed,
  In the darkness heard His voice.

Things above them they divined—
  Thoughts of God, forever true,
And the deathless Compact signed—
  Building *better than they knew*:
Building liberty not planned,
  Law that ampler life controls,
All the greatness of our land
  Lying shadowed in their souls.

In the days that shall succeed,
  Prouder boast no time shall grant
Than to be of them, indeed,
  Children of their Covenant:

OUR HOLIDAYS IN POETRY

Children of the promised day,
   Bound by hope and memory,
Brave, devoted, wise, as they—
   Strong with love's humility.

Florence Earle Coates

Included by permission of the author and Houghton Mifflin Company.

THE PILGRIMS CAME

The Pilgrims came across the sea,
And never thought of you and me;
And yet it's very strange the way
We think of them Thanksgiving Day.

We tell their story old and true
Of how they sailed across the blue,
And found a new land to be free
And built their homes quite near the sea.

Every child knows well the tale
Of how they bravely turned the sail,
And journeyed many a day and night,
To worship God as they thought right.

THANKSGIVING DAY

The people think that they were sad,
And grave; I'm sure that they were glad—
They made Thanksgiving Day—that's fun—
We thank the Pilgrims, every one!

Annette Wynne

Reprinted by permission from "For Days and Days," by Annette Wynne.
Copyright, 1919, by Frederick A. Stokes Company.

PSALM LXV—Selected

Thou visitest the earth, and waterest it:
Thou greatly enrichest it with the river of God, which
      is full of water:
Thou providest them corn, when thou hast so prepared
      the earth.
Thou waterest the ridges thereof abundantly:
Thou settlest the furrows thereof:
Thou makest it soft with showers.
Thou blessest the springing thereof.
Thou crownest the year with thy goodness;
And thy paths drop fatness.
They drop upon the pastures of the wilderness:
And the little hills rejoice on every side.
The pastures are clothed with flocks;
The valleys also are covered with corn;
They shout for joy, they also sing.

The Bible

PSALM XCV—Selected

O come, let us sing unto the Lord:
Let us heartily rejoice in the strength of our salvation.
Let us come before his presence with thanksgiving,
And show ourselves glad in him with psalms.
For the Lord is a great God,
And a great King above all gods.
In his hands are all the corners of the earth:
The strength of the hills is his also.
The sea is his, and he made it:
And his hands prepared the dry land.
O come, let us worship and bow down:
Let us kneel before the Lord our maker.
For he is the Lord our God;
And we are the people of his pasture and the sheep of
    his hand.

The Bible

PSALM C

Make a joyful noise unto the Lord, all ye lands.
Serve the Lord with gladness:
Come before his presence with singing.
Know ye that the Lord he is God:
It is he that hath made us and not we ourselves;
We are his people and the sheep of his pasture.

334

THANKSGIVING DAY

Enter into his gates with thanksgiving,
And into his courts with praise:
Be thankful unto him and bless his name.
For the Lord is gracious; his mercy is everlasting;
And his truth endureth from generation to generation.

The Bible

PSALM CXXXVI—Selected

O give thanks unto the Lord for he is gracious:
For his mercy endureth for ever.
O give thanks unto the God of gods:
For his mercy endureth forever.
O give thanks to the Lord of lords:
For his mercy endureth for ever.
To him who alone doeth great wonders:
For his mercy endureth for ever.
To him that by wisdom made the heavens:
For his mercy endureth for ever.
To him that stretched out the earth above the waters:
For his mercy endureth for ever.
To him that made great lights:
For his mercy endureth for ever.
The sun to rule by day:
For his mercy endureth for ever.

The moon and stars to rule by night:
For his mercy endureth for ever.
O give thanks unto the God of heaven:
For his mercy endureth for ever.

The Bible

PSALM CXLVII—Selected

Sing unto the Lord with thanksgiving;
Sing praise upon the harp unto our God:
Who covereth the heaven with clouds,
Who prepareth rain for the earth,
Who maketh grass to grow upon the mountains,
And herb for the use of men.
He giveth to the beast his food,
And to the young ravens which cry.
Praise the Lord, O Jerusalem;
Praise thy God, O Zion.

The Bible

THE PUMPKIN

Oh, greenly and fair in the lands of the sun,
The vines of the gourd and the rich melon run,
And the rock and the tree and the cottage enfold,
With broad leaves all greenness and blossoms all gold,

336

THANKSGIVING DAY

Like that which o'er Nineveh's prophet once grew,
While he waited to know that his warning was true,
And longed for the storm-cloud, and listened in vain
For the rush of the whirlwind and red-fire rain.

On the banks of the Xenil the dark Spanish maiden
Comes up with the fruit of the tangled vine laden;
And the Creole of Cuba laughs out to behold
Through orange-leaves shining the broad spheres of
      gold;
Yet with dearer delight from his home in the North,
On the fields of his harvest the Yankee looks forth,
Where crook-necks are coiling and yellow fruit shines,
And the sun of September melts down on his vines.

Ah! on Thanksgiving Day, when from East and from
      West,
From North and from South come the pilgrim and
      guest;
When the gray-haired New Englander sees round his
      board
The old broken links of affection restored;
When the care-wearied man seeks his mother once
      more,
And the worn matron smiles where the girl smiled be-
      fore;
What moistens the lip and what brightens the eye,
What calls back the past, like the rich Pumpkin pie?

Oh, fruit loved of boyhood! the old days recalling,
When wood-grapes were purpling and brown nuts were
  falling!
When wild, ugly faces were carved in its skin,
Glaring out through the dark with a candle within!
When we laughed round the corn-heap with hearts all
  in tune,
Our chair a broad pumpkin, our lantern the moon,
Telling tales of the fairy who traveled like steam,
In a pumpkin-shell coach with two rats for her team!

Then thanks for thy present! none sweeter or better
E'er smoked from an oven or circled a platter!
Fairer hands never wrought at a pastry more fine,
Brighter eyes never watched o'er its baking than thine!
And the prayer which my mouth is too full to express,
Swells my heart that thy shadow may never be less,
That the days of thy lot may be lengthened below,
And the fame of thy worth like a pumpkin-vine grow,
And thy life be as sweet, and its last sunset sky
Golden-tinted and fair, as thy own Pumpkin pie!

John Greenleaf Whittier

338

THANKSGIVING DAY

SINGING THE REAPERS HOMEWARD COME

Singing the reapers homeward come, Io! Io!
Merrily singing the harvest home, Io! Io!
    Along the field, along the road,
Where autumn is scattering leaves abroad,
Homeward cometh the ripe last load, Io! Io!

Singers are filling the twilight dim
With cheerful song, Io! Io!
The spirit of song ascends to Him
    Who causeth the corn to grow.
He freely sent the gentle rain,
The summer sun glorified hill and plain,
To golden perfection brought the grain, Io! Io!

Silently, nightly, fell the dew,
Gently the rain, Io! Io!
But who can tell how the green corn grew,
    Or who beheld it grow?
Oh! God, the good, in sun and rain,
He look'd on the flourishing fields of grain,
Till they all appear'd on hill and plain
    Like living gold, Io! Io!

Anonymous

SONG OF THE HARVEST

The glad harvest greets us; brave toiler for bread,
Good cheer! the prospect is brighter ahead;
Like magic, the plentiful sunshine and rain
Have ripened our millions of acres of grain;
And the poorest, the wolf may keep from his door—
There'll be bread and to spare another year more.
       So sing merrily, merrily,
         As we gather it in;
       We will store it away gladly
         In garner and bin.

We hailed with delight, yet tempered with fear,
The corn as it grew from the blade to the ear;
Lest haply, though large is the surplus in store,
That bread might be dearer for twelve months or more.
But the sunshine and rain, how they ripened the grain
That waited the sickle over hillside and plain!
       So sing merrily, merrily,
         As we gather it in;
       We will store it away gladly
         In garner and bin.

Oh, ne'er let us question the Wisdom which guides
Our feet in green pastures, and for us provides;
Who now, as aforetime, His glory displays,

THANKSGIVING   DAY

In the bounty that crowns our autumnal days;
Let the glad tidings echo the continent o'er
There'll be bread and to spare another year more!
      So sing merrily, merrily,
          As we gather it in;
        We will store it away gladly
          In garner and bin.

Henry Stevenson Washburn

A THANKSGIVING

For the wealth of pathless forests,
    Whereon no axe may fall;
For the winds that haunt the branches;
    The young bird's timid call;
For the red leaves dropped like rubies
    Upon the dark green sod;
For the waving of the forests,
    I thank thee, O my God!

For the sound of waters gushing
    In bubbling beads of light;
For the fleets of snow-white lilies
    Firm-anchored out of sight;
For the reeds among the eddies;
    The crystal on the clod;

For the flowing of the rivers,
    I thank Thee, O my God!

For the rosebud's break of beauty
    Along the toiler's way;
For the violet's eye that opens
    To bless the new-born day;
For the bare twigs that in summer
    Bloom like the prophet's rod;
For the blossoming of flowers,
    I thank Thee, O my God!

For the lifting up of mountains,
    In brightness and in dread;
For the peaks where snow and sunshine
    Alone have dared to tread;
For the dark of silent gorges,
    Whence mighty cedars nod;
For the majesty of mountains,
    I thank Thee, O my God!

For the splendor of the sunsets,
    Vast mirrored on the sea;
For the gold-fringed clouds, that curtain
    Heaven's inner mystery;
For the molten bars of twilight,
    Where thought leans, glad, yet awed;
For the glory of the sunsets,
    I thank Thee, O my God!

THANKSGIVING DAY

For the earth, and all its beauty;
    The sky, and all its light;
For the dim and soothing shadows
    That rest the dazzled sight;
For unfading fields and prairies,
    Where sense in vain has trod;
For the world's exhaustless beauty,
    I thank Thee, O my God!

For an eye of inward seeing;
    A soul to know and love;
For these common aspirations,
    That our high heirship prove;
For the hearts that bless each other
    Beneath Thy smile, Thy rod;
For the amaranth saved from Eden
    I thank Thee, O my God!

For the hidden scroll, o'erwritten
    With one dear Name adored;
For the Heavenly in the human;
    The Spirit in the Word;
For the tokens of Thy presence
    Within, above, abroad;
For Thine own great gift of Being,
    I thank Thee, O my God!

Lucy Larcom

Included by permission of The Houghton Mifflin Company.

343

THANKSGIVING DAY

We give Thee thanks, O Lord!
Not for the armed legions, marching in their might,
Not for the glory of the well-earned fight
    Where brave men slay their brothers also brave;
But for the millions of Thy sons who work—
And do Thy task with joy,—and never shirk,
    And deem the idle man a burdened slave:
        For these, O Lord, our thanks!

We give Thee thanks, O Lord!
Not for the turrets of our men-of-war—
The monstrous guns, and deadly steel they pour
    To crush our foes and make them bow the knee;
But for the homely sailors of Thy deep,
The tireless fisher-folk who banish sleep
    And lure a living from the miser sea:
        For these, O Lord, our thanks!

We give Thee thanks, O Lord!
Not for the mighty men who pile up gold,
Not for the phantom millions, bought and sold,
    And all the arrogance of pomp and greed;
But for the pioneers who plow the field,

344

THANKSGIVING   DAY

Make deserts blossom, and the mountain yield
   Its hidden treasures for man's daily need:
     For these, O Lord, our thanks!

   We give Thee thanks, O Lord!
Not for the palaces that wealth has grown,
Where ease is worshipped—duty dimly known,
   And pleasure leads her dance the flowery way;
But for the quiet homes where love is queen
And life is more than baubles, touched and seen,
   And old folks bless us, and dear children play:
     For these, O Lord, our thanks!

Robert Bridges

Included by permission of Collier's, The National Weekly.

THANKSGIVING DAY

Over the river, and through the wood,
   To grandfather's house we go;
     The horse knows the way,
     To carry the sleigh,
   Through the white and drifted snow.

Over the river, and through the wood—
   Oh, how the wind does blow!
     It stings the toes,
     And bites the nose,
   As over the ground we go.

345

Over the river, and through the wood,
   To have a first-rate play.
      Hear the bells ring,
      "Ting-a-ling-ding!"
   Hurrah for Thanksgiving Day!

Over the river and through the wood
   Trot fast, my dapple-gray!
      Spring over the ground
      Like a hunting-hound!
   For this is Thanksgiving Day.

Over the river and through the wood,
   And straight through the barn-yard gate.
      We seem to go
      Extremely slow,—
   It is so hard to wait!

Over the river and through the wood—
   Now grandmother's cap I spy!
      Hurrah for the fun!
      Is the pudding done?
   Hurrah for the pumpkin-pie!

Lydia Maria Child

THANKSGIVING DAY

Brave and high-souled Pilgrims, you who knew no
  fears,
How your words of thankfulness go ringing down
  the years;
May we follow after; like you, work and pray,
And with hearts of thankfulness keep Thanksgiving
  Day.

Annette Wynne

*Reprinted by permission from "For Days and Days," by Annette Wynne.
Copyright, 1919 by Frederick A. Stokes Company.*

THE THANKSGIVING IN BOSTON HARBOR

"Praise ye the Lord!" The psalm to-day
    Still rises on our ears,
Borne from the hills of Boston Bay
    Through five times fifty years,
When Winthrop's fleet from Yarmouth crept
    Out to the open main,
And through the widening waters swept,
    In April sun and rain.
        "Pray to the Lord with fervent lips,"
        The leader shouted, "pray;"

And the prayer arose from all the ships
As faded Yarmouth Bay.

They passed the Scilly Isles that day,
    And May-days came, and June,
And thrice upon the ocean lay
    The full orb of the moon.
And as that day on Yarmouth Bay,
    Ere England sank from view,
While yet the rippling Solent lay
    In April skies of blue,
        "Pray to the Lord with fervent lips,"
            Each morn was shouted, "pray;"
        And prayer arose from all the ships,
            As first in Yarmouth Bay.

Blew warm the breeze o'er western seas,
    Through May-time morns, and June,
Till hailed these souls the Isles of Shoals,
    Low 'neath the summer moon;
And as Cape Ann arose to view,
    And Norman's Woe they passed,
The wood-doves came the white mists through,
    And circled round each mast.
        "Pray to the Lord with fervent lips,"
            Then called the leader, "pray;"
        And prayer arose from all the ships,
            As first in Yarmouth Bay.

348

THANKSGIVING DAY

Above the sea the hill-tops fair—
    God's towers—began to rise,
And odors rare breathe through the air,
    Like the balms of Paradise.
Through burning skies the ospreys flew,
    And near the pine-cooled shores
Danced airy boat and thin canoe,
        To flash of sunlit oars.
            "Pray to the Lord with fervent lips,"
                The leader shouted, "pray;"
            Then prayer arose, and all the ships
                Sailed into Boston Bay.

The white wings folded, anchors down,
    The sea-worn fleet in line,
Fair rose the hills where Boston town
    Should rise from clouds of pine;
Fair was the harbor, summit-walled,
    And placid lay the sea.
"Praise ye the Lord," the leader called;
    "Praise ye the Lord," spake he.
            "Give thanks to God with fervent lips,
                Give thanks to God to-day,"
            The anthem rose from all the ships
                Safe moored in Boston Bay.

                        Hezekiah Butterworth

A THANKSGIVING TO GOD FOR HIS HOUSE

Lord, Thou hast given me a cell
    Wherein to dwell;
A little house, whose humble roof
    Is weather-proof;
Under the spars of which I lie
    Both soft and dry;
Where Thou, my chamber for to ward,
    Hast set a guard
Of harmless thoughts, to watch and keep
    Me, while I sleep.
Low is my porch, as is my fate;
    Both void of state;
And yet the threshold of my door
    Is worn by the poor,
Who thither come, and freely get
    Good words, or meat.
Like as my parlor, so my hall
    And kitchen's small;
A little buttery, and therein
    A little bin,
Which keeps my little loaf of bread
    Unchipped, unflead;
Some brittle sticks of thorn or briar
    Make me a fire,

Close by whose living coal I sit,
    And glow like it.
Lord, I confess too, when I dine,
    The pulse is Thine,
And all those other bits that be
    There placed by Thee:
The worts, the purslain, and the mess
    Of water-cress;
Which of Thy kindness Thou hast sent;
    And my content
Makes those, and my beloved beet,
    To be more sweet.
'Tis Thou that crown'st my glittering hearth
    With guiltless mirth,
And giv'st me wassail bowls to drink,
    Spiced to the brink.
Lord, 'tis Thy plenty-dropping hand
    That soils my land,
And giv'st me, for my bushel sown,
    Twice ten for one;
Thou mak'st my teeming hen to lay
    Her egg each day;
Besides, my healthful ewes to bear
    Me twins each year;
The while the conduits of my kine
    Run cream, for wine:

All these, and better, Thou dost send
      Me, to this end,—
That I should render, for my part,
      A thankful heart;
Which, fired with incense, I resign,
      As wholly Thine;
—But the acceptance, that must be,
      My Christ, by Thee.

Robert Herrick

THAT THINGS ARE NO WORSE, SIRE

From the time of our old Revolution,
      When we threw off the yoke of the King,
Has descended this phrase to remember—
      To remember, to say, and to sing;
'Tis a phrase that is full of a lesson;
      It can comfort and warm like a fire;
It can cheer us when days are the darkest:
      "That things are no worse, O my sire!"

'Twas King George's prime minister said it,
      To the King, who had questioned, in heat,
What he meant by appointing Thanksgiving
      In such days of ill-luck and defeat.
"What's the cause of your day of Thanksgiving?
      Tell me, pray," cried the King in his ire.

THANKSGIVING DAY

Said the minister, "This is the reason—
    That things are no worse, O my sire!"

There was nothing come down, in the story,
    Of the answer returned by the King;
But I think on his throne he sat silent,
    And confessed it a sensible thing;
For there's never a burden so heavy
    That it might not be heavier still;
There is never so bitter a sorrow
    That the cup could not fuller fill.

And what of care and of sadness
    Our life and our duties may bring,
There's always the cause for thanksgiving
    Which the minister told to the King.
'Tis a lesson to sing and to remember;
    It can comfort and warm like a fire,
Can cheer us when days are the darkest—
    "That things are no worse, O my sire!"

Helen Hunt Jackson

CHRISTMAS IN POETRY

God rest ye, merry gentlemen; let nothing you dismay,
For Jesus Christ, our Saviour, was born on Christmas-
day.
The dawn rose red o'er Bethlehem, the stars shone
through the gray,
When Jesus Christ, our Saviour, was born on Christ-
mas-day.

Dinah Maria Muloch Craik

AN ANCIENT CHRISTMAS CAROL

He came all so still
    Where His mother was,
As dew in April
    That falleth on the grass.

He came all so still
    Where His mother lay,
As dew in April
    That falleth on the spray.

He came all so still
    To His mother's bower,
As dew in April
    That falleth on the flower.

Mother and maiden
    Was never none but she!
Well might such a lady
    God's mother be.

Anonymous

AS JOSEPH WAS A-WALKING

As Joseph was a-walking
 He heard an angel sing:—
"This night there shall be born
 Our heavenly King.

"He neither shall be born
 In housen, nor in hall,
Nor in the place of Paradise,
 But in an ox's stall.

"He neither shall be clothéd
 In purple nor in pall;
But in the fair, white linen,
 That usen babies all.

"He neither shall be rockéd
 In silver nor in gold;
But in a wooden cradle
 That rocks on the mould.

"He neither shall be christened
 In white wine nor in red;
But with fair spring water
 With which we were christenéd."

CHRISTMAS

Mary took her baby,
    She dressed Him so sweet,
She laid Him in a manger,
    All there for to sleep.

As she stood over Him
    She heard angels sing,
"O bless our dear Saviour,
    Our heavenly King."

From the Cherry Tree Carol

AUNT MARY
(*A Cornish Christmas Chant*)

Now of all the trees by the king's highway,
    Which do you love the best?
O! the one that is green upon Christmas day,
    The bush with the bleeding breast.
Now the holly with her drops of blood for me;
For that is our dear Aunt Mary's tree.

Its leaves are sweet with our Saviour's name,
    'Tis a plant that loves the poor;
Summer and winter it shines the same,
    Beside the cottage door.
O! the holly with her drops of blood for me;
For that is our kind Aunt Mary's tree.

359

'Tis a bush that the birds will never leave;
　　They sing in it all day long;
But sweetest of all on Christmas eve
　　Is to hear the robins' song.
'Tis the merriest sound upon earth and sea;
For it comes from our own Aunt Mary's tree.

So, of all that grow by the king's highway,
　　I love that tree the best;
'Tis a bower for the birds upon Christmas day,
　　The bush of the bleeding breast.
O! the holly with her drops of blood for me;
For that is our sweet Aunt Mary's tree.

Robert Stephen Hawker

BOOTS AND SADDLES

Our shepherds all
　　As pilgrims have departed,
Our shepherds all
　　Have gone to Bethlehem.
They gladly go
　　For they are all stout-hearted,
They gladly go—
　　Ah, could I go with them!

CHRISTMAS

I am too lame to walk,
  Boots and saddles, boots and saddles,
I am too lame to walk,
  Boots and saddles, mount and ride.

A shepherd stout
  Who sang a catamiaulo,
A shepherd stout
  Was walking lazily.
He heard me speak
  And saw me hobbling after,
He turned and said
  He would give help to me.

"Here is my horse
  That flies along the high-road,
Here is my horse,
  The best in all the towns.
I bought him from
  A soldier in the army,
I got my horse
  By payment of five crowns."

When I have seen
  The Child, the King of Heaven,
When I have seen
  The Child who is God's son,

When to the mother,
     I my praise have given,
When I have finished,
     All I should have done:

     No more shall I be lame,
          Boots and saddles, boots and saddles,
     No more shall I be lame,
     Boots and saddles, mount and ride.

Provençal Nöel of Nicholas Saboly
Included by permission of The H. W. Gray Company.

BRING A TORCH, JEANETTE, ISABELLA

Bring a torch, Jeanette, Isabella!
Bring a torch, to the cradle run!
It is Jesus, good folk of the village;
Christ is born, and Mary's calling;
Ah! Ah! beautiful is the mother;
Ah! Ah! beautiful is her son.

It is wrong when the Child is sleeping,
It is wrong to talk so loud;
Silence, all, as you gather around,
Lest your noise should waken Jesus:
Hush! Hush! see how fast He slumbers;
Hush! Hush! see how fast He sleeps.

CHRISTMAS

Who goes there a-knocking so loudly?
Who goes there a-knocking like that?
Ope your doors, I have here on a plate
Some very good cakes which I am bringing:
Toc! Toc! quickly your doors now open;
Toc! Toc! come let us make good cheer.

Softly to the little stable,
Softly for a moment come;
Look and see how charming is Jesus,
How He is white, His cheeks are rosy.
Hush! Hush! see how the Child is sleeping;
Hush! Hush! see how He smiles in dreams.

Provençal Noël of Nicholas Saboly

CAROL

When the herds were watching
    In the midnight chill,
Came a spotless lambkin
    From the heavenly hill.

Snow was on the mountains,
    And the wind was cold,
When from God's own garden
    Dropped a rose of gold.

When 'twas bitter winter,
    Houseless and forlorn
In a star-lit stable
    Christ the Babe was born.

Welcome, heavenly lambkin;
    Welcome, golden rose;
Alleluia, Baby,
    In the swaddling clothes!

              William Canton

CAROL

Villagers all, this frosty tide,
Let your doors swing open wide,
Though wind may follow, and snow beside,
Yet draw us in by your fire to bide;
    Joy shall be yours in the morning!

Here we stand in the cold and the sleet,
Blowing fingers and stamping feet,
Come from far away you to greet—
You by the fire and we in the street—
    Bidding you joy in the morning!

CHRISTMAS

For ere one half of the night was gone,
Sudden a star has led us on,
Raining bliss and benison—
Bliss to-morrow and more anon,
    Joy for every morning!

Goodman Joseph toiled through the snow—
Saw the star o'er a stable low;
Mary she might not further go—
Welcome thatch, and litter below!
    Joy was hers in the morning!

And then they heard the angels tell
"Who were the first to cry NOWELL?
Animals all, as it befell,
In the stable where they did dwell!
    Joy shall be theirs in the morning!"

Kenneth Grahame

*From "The Wind in the Willows"; Copyright, 1908, by Charles Scrib-
    ner's Sons.*
Included by permission of the publishers.

CAROL

Mary, the mother, sits on the hill,
And cradles Child Jesu, that lies so still;
She cradles Child Jesu, that sleeps so sound,
And the little wind blows the song around.

The little wind blows the mother's words,
"Ei, Jesu, ei," like the song of birds;
"Ei, Jesu, ei," I heard it still,
As I lay asleep at the foot of the hill.

"Sleep, Babe, sleep, mother watch doth keep,
Ox shall not hurt Thee, nor ass, nor sheep;
Dew falls sweet from Thy Father's sky
Sleep, Jesu, sleep! ei, Jesu, ei."

Langdon E. Mitchell

A CAROL FOR TWELFTH DAY

Mark well my heavy doleful tale,
    For Twelfth Day now is come,
And now I must no longer stay,
    And say no word but mum.
For I perforce must take my leave
    Of all my dainty cheer—
Plum porridge, roast beef, and minc'd-pies,
    My strong ale and my beer.

Kind hearted Christmas, now adieu,
    For I with thee must part;
But oh! to take my leave of thee
    Doth grieve me at the heart.

CHRISTMAS

Thou wert an ancient housekeeper,
    And mirth with meat didst keep,
But thou art going out of town
    Which causes me to weep.

Come, butler, fill a brimmer full,
    To cheer my fainting heart,
That to old Christmas I may drink
    Before he does depart.
And let each one that's in the room
    With me likewise condole,
And now to cheer their spirits sad
    Let each one drink a bowl.

And when the same it hath gone round,
    Then fall unto your cheer;
For you well know that Christmas time
    It comes but once a year.
Thanks to my master and my dame
    That do such cheer afford,
God bless them, that each Christmas they
    May furnish so their board.

Old English Carol

CAROL IN PRAISE OF THE HOLLY AND IVY
(Holly and Ivy Made a Great Party)

Holly and Ivy made a great party,
Who should have the mastery
       In lands where they go.

Then spake Holly, "I am fierce and jolly,
I will have the mastery
       In lands where we go."

Then spake Ivy, "I am loud and proud,
And I will have the mastery
       In lands where we go."

Then spake Holly, and bent him down on his knee,
"I pray thee, gentle Ivy,
Essay me no villany
       In the lands where we go."

Fifteenth Century Carol

CAROL OF THE BIRDS

Whence comes this rush of wings afar,
Following straight the Noël star?
Birds from the woods in wondrous flight,
Bethlehem seek this Holy Night.

"Tell us, ye birds, why come ye here,
Into this stable, poor and drear?"
"Hast'ning we seek the new-born King,
And all our sweetest music bring."

Hark how the green-finch bears his part,
Philomel, too, with tender heart,
Chants from her leafy dark retreat
Re, mi, fa, sol, in accents sweet.

Angels and shepherds, birds of the sky,
Come where the Son of God doth lie;
Christ on the earth with man doth dwell,
Join in the shout, Noël, Noël.

Bas-Quercy

CAROL OF THE RUSSIAN CHILDREN

Snow-bound mountains, snow-bound valleys,
Snow-bound plateaus, clad in white,
Fur-robed moujiks, fur-robed nobles,
Fur-robed children, see the light.
Shaggy pony, shaggy oxen,
Gentle shepherds wait the light;
Little Jesus, little Mother,
Good St. Joseph, come this night.

Russian Folk Song

Included by permission of The H. W. Gray Company.

A CATCH BY THE HEARTH

Sing we all merrily
    Christmas is here,
The day that we love best
    Of days in the year.

Bring forth the holly,
    The box, and the bay,
Deck out our cottage
    For glad Christmas-day.

CHRISTMAS

Sing we all merrily,
　　Draw around the fire,
Sister and brother,
　　Grandson and sire.

Anonymous

CEREMONIES FOR CHRISTMAS

Come, bring with a noise,
My merry, merry boys,
The Christmas log to the firing,
While my good dame, she
Bids ye all be free,
And drink to your heart's desiring.

With the last year's brand
Light the new block, and
For good success in his spending,
On your psalteries play,
That sweet luck may
Come while the log is a-tending.

Drink now the strong beer,
Cut the white loaf here,
The while the meat is a-shredding;

371

For the rare mince-pie
And the plums stand by
To fill the paste that's a-kneading.

Robert Herrick

A CHILD'S PRAYER
(*Ex Ore Infantum*)

Little Jesus, wast Thou shy
Once, and just as small as I?
And what did it feel like to be
Out of Heaven, and just like me?
Didst Thou sometimes think of THERE,
And ask where all the angels were?
I should think that I would cry
For my house all made of sky;
I would look about the air,
And wonder where my angels were;
And at waking 'twould distress me—
Not an angel there to dress me!

Hadst Thou ever any toys,
Like us little girls and boys?
And didst Thou play in Heaven with all
The angels, that were not too tall,
With stars for marbles?   Did the things

372

CHRISTMAS

Play CAN YOU SEE ME? through
    their wings?

Didst Thou kneel at night to pray,
And didst Thou join Thy hands, this way
And did they tire sometimes, being young,
And make the prayer seem very long?
And dost Thou like it best, that we
Should join our hands and pray to Thee?
I used to think, before I knew
The prayer not said unless we do.

And did Thy Mother at the night
Kiss Thee and fold the clothes in right?
And didst Thou feel quite good in bed,
Kissed, and sweet, and Thy prayers said?
Thou canst not have forgotten all
That it feels like to be small:
And Thou know'st I cannot pray
To Thee in my father's way—
When Thou wast so little, say,
Could'st Thou talk Thy Father's way?—
So, a little child, come down
And hear a child's tongue like Thy own;
Take me by the hand and walk,
And listen to my baby talk.
To Thy Father show my prayer
(He will look, Thou art so fair),

And say: "O Father, I, Thy son,
Bring the prayer of a little one."

And He will smile, that children's tongue
Hast not changed since Thou wast young!
Francis Thompson

A CHILD'S PRESENT TO HIS CHILD-
SAVIOR

Go, pretty child, and bear this flower
Unto thy little Saviour;
And tell Him, by that bud now blown,
He is the Rose of Sharon known.
When thou hast said so, stick it there
Upon His bib, or stomacher;
And tell Him, for good handsel* too,
That thou hast brought a whistle new,
Made of a clean straight oaten reed,
To charm his cries at time of need.
Tell Him, for coral thou hast none,
But if thou hadst, He should have one;
But poor thou art, and known to be
Even as moneyless as He.
Lastly, if thou canst win a kiss

CHRISTMAS

From those mellifluous lips of His,
Then never take a second on,
To spoil the first impression.

Robert Herrick

*handsel: a gift for good luck.

CHRISTMAS

While shepherds watch'd their flocks by night,
    All seated on the ground,
The angel of the Lord came down,
    And glory shone around.

"Fear not," said he (for mighty dread
    Had seized their troubled mind);
"Glad tidings of great joy I bring
    To you and all mankind.

"To you, in David's town, this day
    Is born of David's line
The Saviour who is Christ the Lord;
    And this shall be the sign:

"The heavenly Babe you there shall find
    To human view display'd,
All meanly wrapt in swathing bands,
    And in a manger laid."

375

Thus spake the Seraph; and forthwith
    Appear'd a shining throng
Of angels, praising God, and thus
    Address'd their joyful song:

"All glory be to God on high,
    And to the earth be peace;
Good-will henceforth from heaven to men
    Begin, and never cease!"

               Nahum Tate

A CHRISTMAS CAROL

Everywhere, everywhere, Christmas to-night!
Christmas in lands of the fir-tree and pine,
Christmas in lands of the palm-tree and vine,
Christmas where snow-peaks stand solemn and white,
Christmas where cornfields lie sunny and bright,
    Everywhere, everywhere, Christmas to-night!

Christmas where children are hopeful and gay,
Christmas where old men are patient and gray,
Christmas where peace, like a dove in its flight,
Broods o'er brave men in the thick of the fight.
    Everywhere, everywhere, Christmas to-night!

CHRISTMAS

For the Christ-child who comes is the Master of all,
No palace too great and no cottage too small;
The angels who welcome Him sing from the height,
"In the City of David, a King in His might."
    Everywhere, everywhere, Christmas to-night!

Then let every heart keep its Christmas within,
Christ's pity for sorrow, Christ's hatred for sin,
Christ's care for the weakest, Christ's courage for right,
Christ's dread of the darkness, Christ's love of the light,
    Everywhere, everywhere, Christmas to-night!

So the stars of the midnight which compass us round
Shall see a strange glory, and hear a sweet sound,
And cry, "Look! the earth is aflame with delight,
O sons of the morning, rejoice at the sight."
    Everywhere, everywhere, Christmas to-night!

Phillips Brook

A CHRISTMAS CAROL

The Christ-child lay on Mary's lap,
    His hair was like a light.
(O weary, weary were the world,
    But here is all aright.)

377

The Christ-child lay on Mary's breast,
  His hair was like a star.
(O stern and cunning are the kings,
  But here the true hearts are.)

The Christ-child lay on Mary's heart,
  His hair was like a fire.
(O weary, weary is the world,
  But here the world's desire.)

The Christ-child stood at Mary's knee,
  His hair was like a crown,
And all the flowers looked up at Him,
  And all the stars looked down.

Gilbert K. Chesterton

Included by permission of the author.

CHRISTMAS CAROL

Christ was born on Christmas day,
Wreathe the holly, twine the bay,
The Babe, the Son, the Holy One of Mary.
Light and life and joy is He,

He is born to set us free,
He is born our Lord to be;
Carol, Christians, joyfully;
The God, the Lord, by all adored forever.

CHRISTMAS

Let the bright berries glow
Everywhere in goodly show,
Light and Life and joy is he,
The Babe, the Son, the Holy One of Mary.

Christian men, rejoice and sing;
'Tis the birthday of our King.
Carol, Christians, joyfully;
The God, the Lord,
By all adored forever.
Night of sadness,
Morn of gladness, **evermore.**
Ever, ever,
After many troubles sore,
Morn of gladness evermore, and evermore.
Midnight scarcely passed and over,
Drawing to the holy morn;
Very early, very early,
Christ was born.
Sing out with bliss,
His name is this:
Emmanuel!
As 'twas foretold,
In the days of old,
By Gabriel.

Thomas Helmore

A CHRISTMAS CAROL

There's a song in the air!
There's a star in the sky!
There's a mother's deep prayer
And a baby's low cry!
    And the star rains its fire while the Beautiful sing,
    For the manger of Bethlehem cradles a king.

There's a tumult of joy
O'er the wonderful birth,
For the virgin's sweet boy
Is the Lord of the earth,
    Ay! the star rains its fire and the Beautiful sing,
    For the manger of Bethlehem cradles a king.

In the light of that star
Lie the ages impearled;
And that song from afar
Has swept over the world.
    Every hearth is aflame, and the Beautiful sing
    In the homes of the nations that Jesus is King.

We rejoice in the light,
And we echo the song
That comes down through the night
From the heavenly throng.

Ay! we shout to the lovely evangel they bring,
And we greet in His cradle our Saviour and King.
Josiah Gilbert Holland

A CHRISTMAS CAROL

God bless the master of this house,
    The mistress also,
And all the little children,
    That round the table go.

And all your kin and folk,
    That dwell both far and near;
I wish you a merry Christmas,
    And a happy New Year.
Old English Carol

A CHRISTMAS CAROL

In the bleak mid-winter
    Frosty wind made moan,
Earth stood hard as iron,
    Water like a stone;
Snow had fallen, snow on snow,
    Snow on snow,
In the bleak mid-winter
    Long ago.

Our God, Heaven cannot hold Him
    Nor earth sustain;
Heaven and earth shall flee away
    When He comes to reign.
In the bleak mid-winter
    A stable-place sufficed
The Lord God Almighty
    Jesus Christ.

Angels and archangels
    May have gathered there,
Cherubim and seraphim
    Thronged the air;
But only His Mother
    In her maiden bliss
Worshipped her Beloved
    With a kiss.

What can I give Him,
    Poor as I am?
If I were a shepherd
    I would bring a lamb,
If I were a Wise Man,
    I would do my part,—
Yet what I can I give Him,
    Give my heart.

Christina G. Rossetti

A CHRISTMAS CAROL

When Christ was born in Bethlehem,
'Twas night but seemed the noon of day:
  The star whose light
  Was and bright,
Shone with unwav'ring ray;
  But one bright star,
  One glorious star
Guided the Eastern Magi from afar.

Then peace was spread throughout the land;
The lion fed beside the lamb;
  And with the kid,
  To pastures led,
The spotted leopard fed
  In peace, in peace
  The calf and bear,
The wolf and lamb reposed together there.

As shepherds watched their flocks by night,
An angel brighter than the sun
  Appeared in air,
  And gently said,
"Fear not, be not afraid,
  Behold, behold,
  Beneath your eyes,
Earth has become a smiling Paradise."

     Translated from the Neapolitan

CHRISTMAS EVE

In holly hedges starving birds
    Silently mourn the setting year;
Upright like silver-plated swords
    The flags stand in the frozen mere.

The mistletoe we still adore
    Upon the twisted hawthorn grows:
In antique gardens hellebore
    Puts forth its blushing Christmas rose.

Shrivell'd and purple, cheek by jowl,
    The hips and haws hang drearily;
Roll'd in a ball the sulky owl
    Creeps far into his hollow tree.

In abbeys and cathedrals dim
    The birth of Christ is acted o'er;
The kings of Cologne worship him,
    Balthazar, Jasper, Melchior.

The shepherds in the field at night
    Beheld an angel glory-clad,
And shrank away with sore afright.
    "Be not afraid," the angel bade.

CHRISTMAS

"I bring good news to king and clown,
　　To you here crouching on the sward;
For there is born in David's town
　　A Saviour, which is Christ the Lord.

"Behold the babe is swathed, and laid
　　Within a manger." Straight there stood
Beside the angel all arrayed
　　A heavenly multitude.

"Glory to God," they sang; "and peace,
　　Good pleasure among men."
The wondrous message of release!
　　Glory to God again!

Hush! Hark! the waits, far up the street!
　　A distant, ghostly charm unfolds,
Of magic music wild and sweet,
　　Anemones and clarigolds.

John Davidson

From "Fleet Street Eclogues." Included by permission of Dodd, Mead and Company.

CHRISTMAS EVE

Oh hush thee, little Dear-my-soul,
　　The evening shades are falling,—
Hush thee, my dear, dost thou not hear
　　The voice of the Master calling?

385

Deep lies the snow upon the earth,
    But all the sky is ringing
With joyous song, and all night long
    The stars shall dance with singing.

Oh hush thee, little Dear-my-soul,
    And close thine eyes in dreaming,
And angels fair shall lead thee where
    The singing stars are beaming.

A Shepherd calls His little lambs,
    And He longeth to caress them;
He bids them rest upon His breast,
    That His tender love may bless them.

So hush thee, little Dear-my-soul,
    Whilst evening shades are falling,
And above the song of the heavenly throng
    Thou shalt hear the Master calling.

Eugene Field

From "Poems of Eugene Field"; copyright, 1910, by Julia S. Field; published by Charles Scribner's Sons. By permission of the publishers.

CHRISTMAS EVE—ANOTHER CEREMONY

Come, guard this night the Christmas-pie,
That the thief, though ne'er so sly,
With his flesh-hooks, don't come nigh
                To catch it.

CHRISTMAS

From him, who alone sits there,
Having his eyes still in his ear,
And a deal of nightly fear
                    To watch it.

ANOTHER TO THE MAIDS

Wash your hands, or else the fire
Will not tend to your desire;
Unwashed hands, ye maidens, know,
Dead the fire, though we blow.

Robert Herrick

CHRISTMAS FOLKSONG

The little Jesus came to town;
The wind blew up, the wind blew down;
Out in the street the wind was bold.
Now who would house Him from the cold?

Then opened wide a stable door
Fain were the rushes on the floor;
The Ox put forth a horned head:
"Come, little Lord, here make Thy bed."

Uprose the Sheep were folded near:
"Thou Lamb of God, come, enter here."
He entered there to rush and reed,
Who was the Lamb of God indeed.

The little Jesus came to town;
With ox and sheep He laid Him down.
Peace to the byre, peace to the fold,
For that they housed Him from the cold.

Lizette Woodworth Reese

Included by permission of Thomas B. Mosher.

A CHRISTMAS HYMN

Once in royal David's city
    Stood a lowly cattle-shed
Where a mother laid her Baby,
    In a manger for His bed.
Mary was that mother mild,
Jesus Christ her little Child.

He came down to earth from heaven,
    Who is God and Lord of all,
And His shelter was a stable,
    And His cradle was a stall.
With the poor, and mean, and lowly
Lived on earth our Saviour holy.

CHRISTMAS

And through all His wondrous childhood,
   He would honour and obey,
Love and watch the lowly mother
   In whose gentle arms He lay.
Christian children, all must be
Mild, obedient, good as He.

For He is our childhood's Pattern,
   Day by day like us He grew;
He was little, weak, and helpless,
   Tears and smiles like us He knew
And He feeleth for our sadness,
And He shareth in our gladness.

And our eyes at last shall see Him,
   Through His own redeeming love,
For that Child so dear and gentle
   Is our Lord in Heaven above;
And He leads His children on
To the place where He is gone.

Not in that poor lowly stable,
   With the oxen standing by,
We shall see Him; but in Heaven,
   Set at God's right hand on high;
When like stars His children crowned,
All in white shall wait around.

Cecil Frances Alexander

CHRISTMAS IN THE HEART

It is Christmas in the mansion,
    Yule-log fires and silken frocks;
It is Christmas in the cottage,
    Mother's filling little socks.

It is Christmas on the highway,
    In the thronging, busy mart;
But the dearest truest Christmas
    Is the Christmas in the heart.

Anonymous

A CHRISTMAS LEGEND

Abroad on a winter's night there ran
Under the starlight, leaping the rills
Swollen with snow-drip from the hills,
    Goat-legged, goat-bearded Pan.

He loved to run on the crisp white floor,
Where black hill-torrents chiselled grooves,
And he loved to print his clean-cut hooves,
    Where none had trod before.

And now he slacked and came to a stand
Beside a river too broad to leap;

390

And as he panted he heard a sheep
    That bleated near at hand.

"Bell-wether, bell-wether, what do you say,
Peace, and huddle your ewes from cold!"
"Master, but ere we went to fold
    Our herdsman hastened away:

"Over the hill came other twain
And pointed away to Bethlehem,
And spake with him, and he followed them,
    And has not come again.

"He dropped his pipe of the river-reed;
He left his scrip in his haste to go;
And all our grazing is under snow,
    So that we cannot feed."

"Left his sheep on a winter's night?"—
Pan folded them with an angry frown.
"Bell-wether, bell-wether, I'll go down
    Where the star shines bright."

Down by the hamlet he met the man.
"Shepherd, no shepherd, thy flock is lorn!"
"Master, no master, a child is born
    Royal, greater than Pan.

"Lo, I have seen; I go to my sheep,
Follow my footsteps through the snow,
But warily, warily see thou go,
    For child and mother sleep."

Into the stable-yard Pan crept,
And there in a manger a baby lay
Beside his mother upon the hay,
    And mother and baby slept.

Pan bent over the sleeping child,
Gazed on him, panting after his run:
And while he wondered, the little one
    Opened his eyes and smiled;

Smiled, and after a little space
Struggled an arm from the swaddling-band,
And raising a tiny dimpled hand,
    Patted the bearded face.

Something snapped in the breast of Pan;
His heart, his throat, his eyes were sore,
And he wished to weep as never before
    Since the world began.

And out he went to the silly sheep,
To the fox on the hill, the fish in the sea,
The horse in the stall, the bird in the tree,
    Asking them how to weep.

CHRISTMAS

They could not teach—they did not know;
The law stands writ for the beast that's dumb
That a limb may ache and a heart be numb,
    But never a tear can flow.

So bear you kindly to-day, O Man,
To all that is dumb and all that is wild,
For the sake of the Christmas Babe who smiled
    In the eyes of great god Pan.
                       Frank Sidgwick

From "Some Verse" by Frank Sidgwick. Published by Sidgwick & Jackson, Ltd.
Included by permission of the author and publishers.

THE CHRISTMAS SILENCE

Hushed are the pigeons cooing low,
    On dusty rafters of the loft;
    And mild-eyed oxen, breathing soft,
Sleep on the fragrant hay below.

Dim shadows in the corner hide;
    The glimmering lantern's rays are shed
    Where one young lamb just lifts his head,
Then huddles 'gainst his mother's side.

Strange silence tingles in the air;
  Through the half-open door a bar
  Of light from one low hanging star
Touches a baby's radiant hair—

No sound—the mother, kneeling, lays
  Her cheek against the little face.
  Oh human love! Oh heavenly grace!
'Tis yet in silence that she prays!

Ages of silence end to-night;
  Then to the long-expectant earth
  Glad angels come to greet His birth
In burst of music, love, and light!

                    Margaret Deland

Included by permission of the author.

CHRISTMAS SONG

Why do bells for Christmas ring?
Why do little children sing?

Once a lovely, shining star,
Seen by shepherds from afar,
Gently moved until its light
Made a manger-cradle bright.

CHRISTMAS

There a darling baby lay
Pillowed soft upon the hay.
And his mother sang and smiled,
"This is Christ, the holy child."

So the bells for Christmas ring,
So the little children sing.

Lydia Avery Coonley Ward

Included by permission of the author.

THE CHRISTMAS TREE IN THE NURSERY

With wild surprise
Four great eyes
In two small heads
From neighboring beds
Looked out—and winked—
And glittered and blinked
At a very queer sight
In the dim dawn-light.
As plain as can be
A fairy tree
Flashes and glimmers
And shakes and shimmers.
Red, green, and blue
Meet their view;

Silver and gold
Sharp eyes behold;
Small moons, big stars;
And jams in jars,
And cakes, and honey,
And thimbles, and money,
Pink dogs, blue cats,
Little squeaking rats,
And candles, and dolls,
And crackers, and polls,
A real bird that sings,
And tokens and favors,
And all sorts of things
For the little shavers.

Four black eyes
Grow big with surprise:
And then grow bigger
When a tiny figure,
Jaunty and airy,
A fairy! a fairy!
From the tree-top cries,
"Open wide! Black Eyes!
Come, children, wake now!
Your joys you may take now!"
Quick as you can think
　　Twenty small toes
　　In four pretty rows,

CHRISTMAS

Like little piggies pink,
All kick in the air—
And before you can wink
The tree stands bare!

Richard Watson Gilder

Included by permission of the author and Houghton Mifflin Company.

THE CHRISTMAS TREES

There's a stir among the trees,
There's a whisper in the breeze,
Little ice-points clash and clink,
Little needles nod and wink,
Sturdy fir-trees sway and sigh—
"Here am I! Here am I!"

"All the summer long I stood
In the silence of the woods.
Tall and tapering I grew;
What might happen well I knew;
For one day a little bird
Sang, and in the song I heard
Many things quite strange to me
Of Christmas and the Christmas tree.

397

"When the sun was hid from sight
In the darkness of the night,
When the wind with sudden fret
Pulled at my green coronet,
Staunch I stood, and hid my fears,
Weeping silent fragrant tears,
Praying still that I might be
Fitted for a Christmas tree.

"Now here we stand
On every hand!
In us a hoard of summer stored,
Birds have flown over us,
Blue sky has covered us,
Soft winds have sung to us,
Blossoms have flung to us
Measureless sweetness,
Now in completeness
We wait."

Mary F. Butts

CRADLE HYMN

Away in a manger, no crib for a bed,
The little Lord Jesus laid down his sweet head.
The stars in the bright sky looked down where he lay–
The little Lord Jesus asleep on the hay.

CHRISTMAS

The cattle are lowing, the baby awakes,
But little Lord Jesus, no crying he makes.
I love thee, Lord Jesus! Look down from the sky,
And stay by my cradle till morning is nigh.

Martin Luther

FEAST O' ST. STEPHEN

Listen all ye, 'tis the Feast o' St. Stephen,
Mind that ye keep it, this holy even.
Open your door and greet ye the stranger,
For ye mind that the wee Lord had naught but
     manger.
                              Mhuire as truagh!
Feed ye the hungry and rest ye the weary,
This ye must do for the sake of Our Mary.
'Tis well that ye mind—ye who sit by the fire—
That the Lord He was born in a dark and cold byre.
                              Mhuire as truagh!

Ruth Sawyer

Included by permission of the author and Harper and Brothers.

THE FIRST CHRISTMAS

Once a little baby lay
Cradled on the fragrant hay,
     Long ago on Christmas;

Stranger bed a babe ne'er found,
Wond'ring cattle stood around,
    Long ago on Christmas.

By the shining vision taught,
Shepherds for the Christ-child sought,
    Long ago on Christmas.
Guided in a starlit way.
Wise men came their gifts to pay,
    Long ago on Christmas.

And to-day the whole glad earth
Praises God for that Child's birth,
    Long ago on Christmas;
For the Life, the Truth, the Way
Came to bless the earth that day,
    Long ago on Christmas.

Emilie Poulsson

FROM FAR AWAY

From far away we come to you.
    The snow in the street, and the wind on the door,
To tell of great tidings, strange and true.
    Minstrels and maids, stand forth on the floor.
        From far away we come to you,
        To tell of great tidings, strange and true.

CHRISTMAS

For as we wandered far and wide,
   The snow in the street, and the wind on the door,
What hap do you deem there should us betide?
   Minstrels and maids, stand forth on the floor.

Under a bent when the night was deep,
   The snow in the street, and the wind on the door,
There lay three shepherds, tending their sheep.
   Minstrels and maids, stand forth on the floor.

"O ye shepherds, what have ye seen,
   The snow in the street, and the wind on the door,
To stay your sorrow and heal your teen?"
   Minstrels and maids, stand forth on the floor.

"In an ox stall this night we saw,
   The snow in the street, and the wind on the door,
A Babe and a maid without a flaw.
   Minstrels and maids, stand forth on the floor.

"There was an old man there beside;
   The snow in the street, and the wind on the door,
His hair was white, and his hood was wide.
   Minstrels and maids, stand forth on the floor.

"And as we gazed this thing upon,
   The snow in the street, and the wind on the door,
Those twain knelt down to the little one.
   Minstrels and maids, stand forth on the floor.

"And a marvellous song we straight did hear,
  The snow in the street, and the wind on the door,
That slew our sorrow and healed our care."
  Minstrels and maids, stand forth on the floor.

News of a fair and marvellous thing,
    The snow in the street, and the wind on the door,
Nowell, Nowell, Nowell, we sing.
  Minstrels and maids, stand forth on the floor.
    From far away we come to you,
    To tell of great tidings, strange and true.

William Morris

GOD REST YE, MERRY GENTLEMEN

God rest ye, merry gentlemen; let nothing you dismay,
For Jesus Christ, our Saviour, was born on Christmas-
        day.
The dawn rose red o'er Bethlehem, the stars shone
        through the gray,
When Jesus Christ, our Saviour, was born on Christ-
        mas-day.

God rest ye, little children; let nothing you affright,
For Jesus Christ, your Saviour, was born this happy
        night;
Along the hills of Galilee the white flocks sleeping lay,

CHRISTMAS

When Christ, the child of Nazareth, was born on
    Christmas-day.

God rest ye, all good Christians; upon this blessed
    morn
The Lord of all good Christians was of a woman born;
Now all your sorrows He doth heal, your sins He takes
    away;
For Jesus Christ, our Saviour, was born on Christmas-
    day.

Dinah Maria Mulock Craik

THE GOLDEN CAROL
(*Of Melchior, Balthazar, and Gaspar, the Three
Kings*)

We saw the light shine out a-far,
    On Christmas in the morning.
And straight we knew Christ's Star it was,
Bright beaming in the morning.
Then did we fall on bended knee,
On Christmas in the morning,
And prais'd the Lord, who'd let us see
His glory at its dawning.

Oh! every thought be of His Name,
    On Christmas in the morning,
Who bore for us both grief and shame,
    Afflictions sharpest scorning.

And may we die (when death shall come),
    On Christmas in the morning,
And see in heav'n, our glorious home,
    The Star of Christmas morning.

Old Carol

GOOD KING WENCESLAS

Good King Wenceslas looked out
    On the Feast of Stephen,
When the snow lay round about,
    Deep, and crisp, and even.

Brightly shone the moon that night
    Though the frost was cruel,
When a poor man came in sight,
    Gath'ring winter fuel.

"Hither, page, and stand by me,
    If thou know'st it, telling,
Yonder peasant, who is he?
    Where and what his dwelling?"

"Sire, he lives a good league hence,
    Underneath the mountain;
Right against the forest fence,
    By Saint Agnes' fountain."

404

CHRISTMAS

"Bring me flesh, and bring me wine,
  Bring me pine-logs hither;
Thou and I shall see him dine,
  When we bear them thither."

Page and monarch, forth they went,
  Forth they went together;
Through the rude wind's wild lament
  And the bitter weather.

"Sire, the night is darker now,
  And the wind blows stronger;
Fails my heart, I know not how,
  I can go no longer."

"Mark my footsteps, good my page;
  Tread thou in them boldly:
Thou shalt find the winter rage
  Freeze thy blood less coldly."

In his master's steps he trod,
  Where the snow lay dinted;
Heat was in the very sod
  Where the saint had printed.

Therefore, Christian men, be sure,
  Wealth or rank possessing,
Ye who now will bless the poor,
  Shall yourselves find blessing.

Translated from the Latin by J. M. Neale

JOSEPH, JESUS AND MARY

Joseph, Jesus and Mary
    Were travelling for the west,
When Mary grew a-tired,
    She might sit down and rest.

They travelled further and further,
    The weather being so warm,
Till they came unto a husbandman
    A-sowing of his corn.

"Come, husbandman," cried Jesus,
    "Throw all your seed aside,
And carry home as ripened corn
    That you have sowed this tide.

"For to keep your wife and family
    From sorrow, grief and pain,
And keep Christ in remembrance
    Till seed time comes again."

From a Gypsy Carol

THE LEAST OF CAROLS

Loveliest dawn of gold and rose
Steals across undrifted snows;
In brown, rustling oak leaves stir

CHRISTMAS

Squirrel, nuthatch, woodpecker;
Brief their matins, but, by noon,
All the sunny wood's a-tune:
Jays, forgetting their harsh cries,
Pipe a spring note, clear and true;
Wheel on angel wings of blue,
Trumpeters of Paradise;
Then the tiniest feathered thing,
All a-flutter, tail and wing,
Gives himself to caroling:

"Chick-a-dee-dee, chick-a-dee!
Jesulino, hail to thee!
Lowliest baby born to-day,
Pillowed on a wisp of hay;
King no less of sky and earth,
            And singing sea;
Jesu! Jesu! most and least!
For the sweetness of thy birth
Every little bird and beast,
Wind and wave and forest tree,
Praises God exceedingly,
            Exceedingly."

Sophie Jewett

From "The Poems of Sophie Jewett." Included by permission of the Thomas Y. Crowell Company.

A LEGEND

Christ, when a child, a garden made,
    And many roses flourished there,
He watered them three times a day,
    To make a garland for his hair.

And when in time the roses bloomed
    He called the children in to share;
They tore the flowers from every stem
    And left the garden stript and bare.

"How wilt thou weave thyself a crown
    Now that thy roses all are dead?"
"Ye have forgotten that the thorns
    Are left for me," the Christ-child said.

They plaited then a crown of thorns
    And laid it rudely on his head.
A garland for his forehead made
    For roses drops of blood instead.

Tschaikovsky

By courtesy of G. Schirmer, Inc.

LONG, LONG AGO

Winds thru the olive trees
   Softly did blow,
Round little Bethlehem
   Long, long ago.

Sheep on the hillside lay
   Whiter than snow
Shepherds were watching them,
   Long, long ago.

Then from the happy sky,
   Angels bent low
Singing their songs of joy,
   Long, long ago.

For in a manger bed,
   Cradled we know,
Christ came to Bethlehem,
   Long, long ago.

Anonymous

LORDINGS, LISTEN TO OUR LAY

Lordings, listen to our lay—
We have come from far away
　　To seek Christmas;
In this mansion we are told
He His yearly feast doth hold:
　　'Tis to-day!
May joy come from God above,
To all those who Christmas love.

Old Carol

MARCH OF THE THREE KINGS

This high-way
Beheld at break of day
Three Eastern Kings go by upon their journey.
This high-way
Beheld at break of day
Three Eastern Kings go by in rich array.
With courage high
All their guards passed by,
Their knights-at-arms with the squires and the pages.
With courage high
All their guards passed by,
With gilded armor shining like the sky.

CHRISTMAS

Wondering then,
I watched the mighty men,
I stood amazed as the knights were passing.
Wondering then,
I watched the mighty men,
And as they passed I followed them again.
They journeyed far
To the guiding star
That shone where Jesus was lying in a manger.
And far away
Where the Christ Child lay
They found the shepherds come to watch and pray.

Gaspard old
Had brought a gift of gold.
He said, "My Lord, Thou art the King of Glory."
Gaspard old
Gave Christ his gift of gold,
And that this Child would conquer death, he told.
Then incense sweet
At the Christ Child's feet
King Melchior placed, saying, "Thou art God of
armies."
Although He lies
Here in humble guise,
This little Child is God of earth and skies."

"You will die;
For You, my Lord, I cry,"
Wept Balthazar, his gifts of myrrh presenting.
"You will die
And in a tomb will lie,
For on a cross you will be lifted high."
All we to-day
To the Child must pray,
Who came to earth with His gifts of peace and blessing,
To Him we pray
And our homage pay
And with the Kings we march along the way.

Old Provençal Carol

Included by permission of The H. W. Gray Company.

NATIVITY SONG

The beautiful mother is bending
Low where her baby lies,
Helpless and frail, for her tending;
But she knows the glorious eyes.

The mother smiles and rejoices
While the baby laughs in the hay;
She listens to heavenly voices:
"The child shall be king, one day."

412

CHRISTMAS

O dear little Christ in the manger,
　　Let me make merry with thee.
O King, in my hour of danger,
　　Wilt thou be strong for me?

*Adapted from the Latin of Jacopone da Todi
by Sophie Jewett*

*From "The Poems of Sophie Jewett." Included by permission of the
Thomas Y. Crowell Company.*

THE NEIGHBORS OF BETHLEHEM

Good neighbor, tell me why that sound,
That noisy tumult rising round,
Awaking all in slumber lying?
Truly disturbing are these cries,
All through the quiet village flying,
O come ye shepherds, wake, arise!

What, neighbor, then do ye not know
God hath appeared on earth below
And now is born in manger lowly!
In humble guise he came this night,
Simple and meek, this infant holy,
Yet how divine in beauty bright.

Good neighbor, I must make amend,
Forthwith to bring Him will I send,
And Joseph with the gentle Mother.

413

When to my home these three I bring,
Then will it far outshine all other,
A palace fair for greatest king!

Thirteenth Century French Carol

Included by permission of The H. W. Gray Company.

NEW PRINCE, NEW POMP

Behold a little, tender Babe,
In freezing winter night,
In homely manger trembling lies;
Alas! a piteous sight.
The inns are full; no man will yield
This little Pilgrim bed;
But forced he is with silly beasts
In crib to shroud his head.

Weigh not his crib, his wooden dish,
Nor beasts that by him feed;
Weigh not his mother's poor attire,
Nor Joseph's simple weed.
This stable is a Prince's court,
The crib his chair of state;
The beasts are parcel of his pomp,
The wooden dish his plate.

414

CHRISTMAS

The persons in that poor attire
His royal liv'ries wear;
The Prince himself is come from heav'n;
This pomp is praised there.
With joy approach, O Christian wight!
Do homage to thy King;
And highly praise this humble pomp,
Which he from Heav'n doth bring.

Robert Southwell

NOW THRICE WELCOME CHRISTMAS

Now thrice welcome Christmas,
    Which brings us good-cheer,
Minced pies and plum-porridge,
    Good ale and strong beer;
With pig, goose, and capon,
    The best that can be,
So well doth the weather
    And our stomachs agree.

Observe how the chimneys
    Do smoke all about,
The cooks are providing
    For dinner no doubt;

CHRISTMAS

But those on whose tables
      No victuals appear,
O may they keep Lent
      All the rest of the year!

With holly and ivy
      So green and so gay,
We deck up our houses
      As fresh as the day,
With bays and rosemary,
      And laurel complete,
And everyone now
      Is a king in conceit.

Poor Richard's Almanack, 1695

O LITTLE TOWN OF BETHLEHEM

O little town of Bethlehem,
      How still we see thee lie!
Above thy deep and dreamless sleep
      The silent hours go by.
Yet in thy dark street shineth
      The everlasting Light;
The hopes and fears of all the years
      Are met in thee to-night.

CHRISTMAS

O morning stars, together
    Proclaim the holy birth!
And praises sing to God the King,
    And peace to men on earth.
For Christ is born of Mary
    And gathered all above,
While mortals sleep the Angels keep
    Their watch of wondering love.

How silently, how silently,
    The wondrous gift is given!
So God imparts to human hearts
    The blessings of His Heaven.
No ear may hear His coming;
    But in this world of sin,
Where meek souls will receive Him still,
    The dear Christ enters in.

Where children pure and happy
    Pray to the blessed Child,
Where Misery cries out to Thee,
    Son of the Mother mild.
Where Charity stands watching,
    And Faith holds wide the door,
The dark night wakes, the glory breaks,
    And Christmas comes once more.

O holy child of Bethlehem,
　　Descend to us we pray!
Cast out our sin and enter in,
　　Be born in us to-day.
We hear the Christmas angels
　　The great glad tidings tell;
O, come to us, abide with us,
　　O Lord Emmanuel!

Phillips Brooks

OLD CHRISTMAS

All you that in His house be here,
　　Remember Christ that for us dy'd,
And spend away with modest cheere
　　In loving sort this Christmas-tide.

And whereas plenty God hath sent,
　　Give frankly to your friends in love:
The bounteous mind is freely bent,
　　And never will a niggard prove.

Our table's spread within the hall,
　　I know a banquet is at hand,
And friendly sort to welcome all
　　That will unto their cacklings stand.

CHRISTMAS

The maids are bonny girles, I see,
    Who have provided much good cheere,
Which at my dame's commandment be
    To set it on the table here.

For I have here two knives in store
    To lend to him that wanteth one;
Commend my wits, good lads, therefore,
    That come now hither having none.

For if I should, no Christmas pye
    Would fall, I doubt, unto my share;
Wherefore I will my manhood try
    To fight a battle if I dare.

For pastry crust, like castle walls,
    Stands braving me unto my face;
I am not well until it falls,
    And I made captain of the place.

The prunes so lovely look on me,
    I cannot choose but venture on:
One pye-meat spiced brave I see,
    One which, I must not leave alone.

Old English Carol

OLD CHRISTMAS RETURNED

All you that to feasting and mirth are inclined,
Come here is good news for to pleasure your mind,
Old Christmas is come for to keep open house,
He scorns to be guilty of starving a mouse:
Then come, boys, and welcome for diet the chief,
Plum-pudding, goose, capon, minced pies, and roast
      beef.

The holly and ivy about the walls wind
And show that we ought to our neighbors be kind,
Inviting each other for pastime and sport,
And where we best fare, there we most do resort;
We fail not of victuals, and that of the chief,
Plum-pudding, goose, capon, minced pies, and roast
      beef.

All travellers, as they do pass on their way,
At gentlemen's halls are invited to stay,
Themselves to refresh, and their horses to rest,
Since that he must be Old Christmas's guest;
Nay, the poor shall not want, but have for relief,
Plum-pudding, goose, capon, minced pies, and roast
      beef.

Old English Carol

420

OUR JOYFUL FEAST

So, now is come our joyful feast,
    Let every soul be jolly!
Each room with ivy leaves is drest,
    And every post with holly.
Though some churls at our mirth repine,
Round your brows let garlands twine,
Drown sorrow in a cup of wine,
    And let us all be merry!

Now all our neighbours' chimneys smoke,
    And Christmas logs are burning;
Their ovens with baked meats do choke,
    And all their spits are turning.
Without the door let sorrow lie,
And if for cold it hap to die,
We'll bury it in Christmas pie,
    And evermore be merry!

George Wither

THE SHEPHERD BOYS

The shepherd boys
Have met in their assembly.
The shepherd boys
Have thought what they should do.

421

When in their gathering each one had spoken
Telling his wish, they all boldly determined
              To find
        The King of all mankind.

              So in a band
        They set forth on their journey,
              All in a band
        In the wind and the storm.
For the brave shepherd lads reared in the mountains
Never are daunted by trouble or danger.
              They go
        And leave their homes below.

        Our shepherds all
        When it three o'clock sounded,
        Our shepherds all
        Have come there to the stall.
Hats in their hands they run now to the manger,
Hastening to bless and praise Mary the mother.
              They bend
        Before the child their friend.

        They leave for him
        Some cheese, their birthday present,
        They leave for him
        A full dozen of eggs.

Then Joseph said to them: "Be faithful shepherds,
Go whence you came and be safe on your journey.
Good men
Go to your home again."

Provençal Noël of Nicholas Saboly

Included by permission of The H. W. Gray Company.

THE SHEPHERD WHO STAYED

There are in Paradise
Souls neither great nor wise,
Yet souls who wear no less
The crown of faithfulness.

My master bade me watch the flock by night;
My duty was to stay. I do not know
What thing my comrades saw in that great light,
I did not heed the words that bade them go,
I know not were they maddened or afraid;
I only know I stayed.

The hillside seemed on fire; I felt the sweep
Of wings above my head; I ran to see
If any danger threatened these my sheep.
What though I found them folded quietly,
What though my brother wept and plucked my sleeve,
They were not mine to leave.

Thieves in the wood and wolves upon the hill,
My duty was to stay. Strange though it be,
I had no thought to hold my mates, no will
To bid them wait and keep the watch with me.
I had not heard that summons they obeyed;
    I only know I stayed.

Perchance they will return upon the dawn
With word of Bethlehem and why they went.
I only know that watching here alone,
I know a strange content.
I have not failed that trust upon me laid;
    I ask no more—I stayed.

Theodosia Garrison

THE SHEPHERDS HAD AN ANGEL

The shepherds had an angel,
    The wise men had a star;
But what have I, a little child,
    To guide me home from far,
Where glad stars sing together,
    And singing angels are?

Lord Jesus is my Guardian,
    So I can nothing lack;

CHRISTMAS

The lambs lie in His bosom
    Along life's dangerous track:
The wilful lambs that go astray
    He, bleeding, brings them back.

Those shepherds thro' the lonely night
    Sat watching by their sheep,
Until they saw the heav'nly host
    Who neither tire nor sleep,
All singing Glory, glory,
    In festival they keep.

Christ watches me, His little lamb,
    Cares for me day and night,
That I may be His own in heav'n;
    So angels clad in white
Shall sing their Glory, glory,
    For my sake in the height.

Lord, bring me nearer day by day,
    Till I my voice unite,
And sing my Glory, glory,
    With angels clad in white.
All Glory, glory, giv'n to Thee,
    Thro' all the heav'nly height.

Christina G. Rossetti

SIGNS OF CHRISTMAS

When on the barn's thatch'd roof is seen
The moss in tufts of liveliest green;
When Roger to the wood pile goes,
And, as he turns, his fingers blows;
When all around is cold and drear,
Be sure that Christmas-tide is near.

When up the garden walk in vain
We seek for Flora's lovely train;
When the sweet hawthorn bower is bare,
And bleak and cheerless is the air;
When all seems desolate around,
Christmas advances o'er the ground.

When Tom at eve comes home from plough,
And brings the mistletoe's green bough,
With milk-white berries spotted o'er,
And shakes it the sly maids before,
Then hangs the trophy up on high,
Be sure that Christmas-tide is nigh.

When Hal, the woodman, in his clogs,
Bears home the huge unwieldy logs,
That, hissing on the smouldering fire,

426

CHRISTMAS

Flame out at last a quiv'ring spire;
When in his hat the holly stands,
Old Christmas musters up his bands.

When cluster'd round the fire at night,
Old William talks of ghost and sprite,
And, as a distant out-house gate
Slams by the wind, they fearful wait,
While some each shadowy nook explore,
Then Christmas pauses at the door.

When Dick comes shiv'ring from the yard,
And says the pond is frozen hard,
While from his hat, all white with snow,
The moisture, trickling, drops below,
While carols sound, the night to cheer,
Then Christmas and his train are here.

Edwin Lees

SING, SING FOR CHRISTMAS

Sing, sing for Christmas!
   Welcome happy day!
For Christ is born our Saviour,
   To take our sins away.

Sing, sing a joyful song,
　　Loud and clear to-day;
To praise our Lord and Saviour,
　　Who in the manger lay.

Tell, tell the story
　　Of the wondrous night,
When shepherds who were watching
　　Their flocks till morning light,
Saw angel hosts from heav'n,
　　Heard the angel voice,
And so were told the tidings
　　Which make the world rejoice.

Soft, softly shining,
　　Stars were in the sky,
And silver fell the moonlight
　　On hill and mountain high,
When suddenly the night
　　Outshone the bright mid-day,
With angel hosts who, herald
　　The reign of peace for aye.

Hark, hear them singing,
　　Singing in the sky,
Of worship, honor, glory,
　　And praise to God on high!
Peace, peace, good-will to men!
　　Born the child from heaven!

CHRISTMAS

The Christ, the Lord, the Saviour,
    The Son to you is given!

Sing, sing for Christmas!
    Echo, earth, the cry
Of worship, honor, glory,
    And praise to God on high!
Sing, sing the joyful song,
    Let it never cease,
Of glory in the highest,
    On earth, good-will and peace.

J. H. Egar

THE SINGERS IN THE SNOW

God bless the master of this house
    And all that are therein,
And to begin the Christmas tide
    With mirth now let us sing.

For the Saviour of all the people
    Upon this time was born,
Who did from death deliver us,
    When we were left forlorn.

Then let us all most merry be,
    And sing with cheerful voice,

For we have good occasion now
　　This time for to rejoice.
　　　　　For, etc.

Then put away contention all
　　And fall no more at strife,
Let every man with cheerfullness
　　Embrace his loving wife.
　　　　　For, etc.

With plenteous food your houses store,
　　Provide some wholesome cheer,
And call your friends together,
　　That live both far and near.
　　　　　For, etc.

Then let us all most merry be,
　　Since that we are come here,
And we do hope before we part
　　To taste some of your beer.
　　　　　For, etc.

Your beer, your beer, your Christmas beer.
　　That seems to be so strong;
And we do wish that Christmas tide
　　Was twenty times so long.
　　　　　For, etc.

CHRISTMAS

Then sing with voices cheerfully,
   For Christ this time was born,
Who did from death deliver us,
   When we were left forlorn.
           For, etc.

          Old English Carol

SONG OF A SHEPHERD BOY AT BETHLEHEM

Sleep, Thou little Child of Mary,
   Rest Thee now.
Though these hands be rough from shearing
   And the plow,
Yet they shall not ever fail Thee,
When the waiting nations hail Thee,
Bringing palms unto their King.
   Now—I sing.

Sleep, Thou little Child of Mary,
   Hope divine.
If Thou wilt but smile upon me,
   I will twine
Blossoms for Thy garlanding.
Thou'rt so little to be King.
   God's Desire!
   Not a brier

431

Shall be left to grieve thy brow;
    Rest Thee now.

Sleep, Thou little Child of Mary,
    Some fair day
Wilt Thou, as Thou wert a brother,
    Come away
Over hills and over hollow?
All the lambs will up and follow,
Follow but for love of Thee.
    Lov'st Thou me?

Sleep, Thou little Child of Mary,
    Rest Thee now.
I that watch am come from sheep-stead
    And from plough.
Thou wilt have disdain of me
When Thou'rt lifted, royally,
Very high for all to see:
    Smilest Thou?

Josephine Preston Peabody

Included by permission of the author.

THE SONG OF THE CHRISTMAS TREE

Oho for the woods where I used to grow,
The home of the lonely owl and crow!
I spread my arms to shelter all
The creatures shy, both large and small.

432

CHRISTMAS

I sang for joy to the friends I knew:
The sunshine, rain, and the sky so blue.
Oho for the forest!   Oho for the hills!
Oho for the ripples of murmuring rills!
    Oho, sing I, oho!

Oho for the hall where I now hold sway,
The home of the happy children gay!
I spread my arms with gifts for all,
From father big to baby small.
I sing for joy to these hearts that glow—
Of manger bed, and the Child we know.
Oho for the holly!   Oho for the light!
Oho for the mistletoe's berries so white!
    Oho, sing I, oho!

Blanche Elizabeth Wade

Included by permission of the author and The St. Nicholas Magazine.

STOCKING SONG ON CHRISTMAS EVE

Welcome Christmas! heel and toe,
Here we wait thee in a row.
Come, good Santa Claus, we beg
Fill us tightly, foot and leg.

433

Fill us quickly ere you go,—
Fill us till we overflow,
That's the way! and leave us more
Heaped in piles upon the floor.

Little feet that ran all day
Twitch in dreams of merry play,
Little feet that jumped at will
Lie all pink and white and still.

See us, how we lightly swing,
Hear us how we try to sing,
Welcome Christmas! heel and toe,
Come and fill us ere you go!

Here we hang till some one nimbly
Jumps with treasures down the chimney.
Bless us! how he'll tickle us!
Funny old Saint Nicholas.

Mary Mapes Dodge

THE STORY OF THE SHEPHERD

It was the very noon of night: the stars above the fold,
More sure than clock or chiming bell, the hour of mid-
        night told:

CHRISTMAS

When from the heav'ns there came a voice, and forms
        were seen to shine
Still bright'ning as the music rose with light and love
        divine.
With love divine, the song began; there shone a light
        serene:
O, who hath heard what I have heard, or seen what I
        have seen?

O ne'er could nightingale at dawn salute the rising
        day
With sweetness like that bird of song in his immortal
        lay:
O ne'er were woodnotes heard at eve by banks with
        poplar shade
So thrilling as the concert sweet by heav'nly harpings
        made;
For love divine was in each chord, and filled each
        pause between:
O, who hath heard what I have heard, or seen what I
        have seen?

I roused me at the piercing strain, but shrunk as from
        the ray
Of summer lightning: all around so bright the splen-
        dour lay.
For oh, it mastered sight and sense, to see that glory
        shine,

To hear that minstrel in the clouds, who sang of Love
      Divine,
To see that form with bird-like wings, of more than
      mortal mien:
O, who hath heard what I have heard, or seen what I
      have seen?

When once the rapturous trance was past, that so my
      sense could blind,
I left my sheep to Him whose care breathed in the
      western wind:
I left them, for instead of snow, I trod on blade and
      flower,
And ice dissolved in starry rays at morning's gracious
      hour,
Revealing where on earth the steps of Love Divine had
      been:
O, who hath heard what I have heard, or seen what I
      have seen?

I hasted to a low-roofed shed, for so the Angel bade;
And bowed before the lowly rack where Love Divine
      was laid:
A new-born Babe, like tender Lamb, with Lion's
      strength there smiled;
For Lion's strength immortal might, was in that new-
      born Child;

436

That Love Divine in child-like form had God for ever
      been:
O, who hath heard what I have heard, or seen what I
      have seen?

Translated from the Spanish

'TWAS JOLLY, JOLLY WAT

'Twas jolly, jolly Wat, my foy,
He was a goodman's shepherd boy,
    And he sat by his sheep
    On the hill-side so steep,
      And piped this song,
        Ut hoy! Ut hoy!
   O merry, merry sing for joy,
        Ut hoy!

A'down from Heav'n that is so high
There came an angel companye,
    And on Bethlehem hill
    Thro' the night-tide so still
      Their song out-rang:
        On high, On high,
   O glory be to God on high,
        On high!

437

Now must Wat go where Christ is born,
Yea, go and come again to-morn.
  And my pipe it shall play,
  All my heart it doth say
    To Shepherd King:
      Ut hoy! Ut hoy!
  O merry, merry sing for joy,
    Ut hoy!

O peace on earth, good will to men
The angels sang again, again,
  For to you was He born
  On this Christmas morn,
    So sing we all:
      On high, On high,
  O glory be to God on high,
    On high!

Jesu my King, it's naught for Thee,
A bob of cherries, one, two, three,
  But my tar-box and ball,
  And my pipe, I give all
    To Thee, my King.
      Ut hoy! Ut hoy!
  O merry, merry sing for joy,
    Ut hoy!

CHRISTMAS

Farewell, herd-boy, saith Mary mild.
Thanks, jolly Wat, smiled Mary's child,
    For fit gift for a king
    Is your heart in the thing.
      So pipe you well,
        For joy, for joy!
O merry, merry sing for joy,
      Ut hoy!

C. W. Stubbs

THE WASSAIL SONG

Here we come a-wassailing
    Among the leaves so green,
Here we come a-wandering
    So fair to be seen.

Love and joy come to you
    And to your wassail too,
And God bless you, and send you
    A happy New Year.

We are not daily beggars
    That beg from door to door,
But we are neighbours' children
    That you have seen before.

Good Master and good Mistress,
    As you sit by the fire,
Pray think of us poor children
    Who are wandering in the mire.

Bring us out a table
    And spread it with a cloth;
Bring us out a mouldy cheese
    And some of your Christmas loaf.

God bless the master of this house,
    Likewise the mistress too;
And all the little children
    That round the table go.

Old Devonshire Carol

Included by permission of The H. W. Gray Company.

WASSAIL SONG

Wassail! wassail! all round the town,
For the cup is white and the ale is brown,
    For it's our wassail, and 'tis your wassail,
    And 'tis joy come to our jolly wassail!

The cup is made of the ashen tree,
And the ale is made of the best barley,
    For it's our wassail, and 'tis your wassail,
    And 'tis joy come to our jolly wassail!

CHRISTMAS

O maid, fair maid in Holland smock,
Come ope the door and turn the lock,
    For it's our wassail, and 'tis your wassail,
    And 'tis joy come to our jolly wassail!

O master, mistress, that sit by the fire,
Consider us poor travellers all in the mire.
    For it's our wassail, and 'tis your wassail,
    And 'tis joy come to our jolly wassail!

Put out the ale and raw milk cheese,
And then you shall see how happy we be's,
    For it's our wassail, and 'tis your wassail,
    And 'tis joy come to our jolly wassail!

Old Somersetshire Carol

WASSAILER'S SONG

Wassail! Wassail! all over the town,
Our bread it is white, our ale it is brown;
Our bowl is made of a maplin tree;
We be good fellows all;—I drink to thee.

Here's to our horse, and to his right ear,
God send master a happy new year;
A happy new year as ever he did see,—
With my wassail bowl I drink to thee.

441

Here's to our mare, and to her right eye,
God send our mistress a good Christmas pie;
A good Christmas pie as e'er I did see,—
With my wassailing bowl I drink to thee.

Here's to our cow, and to her long tail,
God send our master us never may fail
Of a cup of good beer: I pray you draw near,
And our jolly wassail it's then you shall hear.

Be here any maids? I suppose here be some;
 Sure they will not let young men stand on the cold stone
Sing hey, O, maids; come trole back the pin,
And the fairest maid in the house let us all in.

Come, butler, come, bring us a bowl of the best;
I hope your souls in heaven will rest;
But if you do bring us a bowl of the small,
Then, down fall butler, and bowl and all.

Robert Southwell

WE THREE KINGS

We Three Kings of Orient are,
Bearing gifts we traverse afar,
        Field and fountain,
        Moor and mountain,
Following yonder star.

Chorus

    O Star of wonder, Star of night,
    Star with Royal Beauty bright,
        Westward leading,
        Still proceeding,
    Guide us to Thy perfect Light.

Gaspard: Born a king on Bethlehem plain,
    Gold I bring to crown Him again;
        King forever,
        Ceasing never
    Over us all to reign.

Chorus: O Star of wonder. . . .

Melchior: Frankincense to offer have I,
    Incense owns a deity nigh;
        Prayer and praising
        All men raising,
    Worship Him God on high.

Chorus: O Star of wonder. . . .

Balthazar: Myrrh is mine; its bitter perfume
    Breathes a life of gathering gloom;
        Sorrowing, sighing,
        Bleeding, dying,
    Sealed in a stone-cold tomb.

443

Chorus: O Star of wonder. . . .

Glorious now behold Him arise,
King and God, and Sacrifice;
   Heav'n sings Allelujah:
   Allelujah,
The earth replies.

J. H. Hopkins, Jr.

WHEN THE CHRIST CHILD CAME

'Twas Christmas Eve, the snow
   Lay deep upon the ground,
The peasants' fire burnt low,
   The children shivered round.

Their scanty evening meal,
   Lay on the humble board,
But all, with thankful hearts,
   Arose and blessed the Lord.

Hark! someone knocks without,
   The peasant opens the door—
Who wanders late to-night
   Across the bitter moor?

CHRISTMAS

Amid the winter storm
    There in the dark He stands,
A Child with wistful eyes
    And frozen, lifted hands.

The peasant took him in,
    The children wond'ring gaze—
He wiped away the snows,
    And warmed Him by the blaze.

There on the seat they loved,
    The dear, dead mother's chair,
They broke the bread and gave,
    Each of his scanty share.

But while on beds of straw
    That night they sleeping lay,
The Child arose and blessed them,
    And softly went His way.

Now for each good that comes,
    When life seems doubly drear,
They fold their hands and say,
    "The Christ Child hath been here."
        Frederick E. Weatherly

Included by permission of the author.

WHILE STARS OF CHRISTMAS SHINE

While stars of Christmas shine,
　　Lighting the skies,
Let only loving looks,
　　Beam from our eyes.

While bells of Christmas ring,
　　Joyous and clear,
Speak only happy words,
　　All love and cheer.

Give only loving gifts,
　　And in love take;
Gladden the poor and sad
　　For love's dear sake.

Emilie Poulsson

INDEX OF AUTHORS

INDEX OF AUTHORS

448

INDEX OF AUTHORS

449

INDEX OF AUTHORS

INDEX OF AUTHORS

INDEX OF AUTHORS

INDEX OF AUTHORS

453

INDEX OF AUTHORS

INDEX OF AUTHORS

INDEX OF AUTHORS

456

INDEX OF AUTHORS

INDEX OF AUTHORS

INDEX OF AUTHORS

INDEX OF AUTHORS

INDEX OF AUTHORS

461

INDEX OF AUTHORS

TITLE INDEX

TITLE INDEX

TITLE INDEX

465

TITLE INDEX

TITLE INDEX

467

TITLE INDEX

TITLE INDEX

469

TITLE INDEX

470

TITLE INDEX

INDEX OF FIRST LINES

INDEX OF FIRST LINES

INDEX OF FIRST LINES

INDEX OF FIRST LINES

476

INDEX OF FIRST LINES

477

INDEX OF FIRST LINES

INDEX OF FIRST LINES

INDEX OF FIRST LINES